Creativity Defined

From Select Passages in Literature

Edited by

Blake Bazel, M.S.

Including: Afterword with MARISOL BLANCO'S poem "Odyssey"

AuthorHouse™
1663 Liberty Drive, Suite 200
Bloomington, IN 47403
www.authorhouse.com
Phone: 1-800-839-8640

© *2008 Blake Bazel, M.S.. All rights reserved.*

No part of this book may be reproduced, stored in a retrieval system, or transmitted by any means without the written permission of the author.

First published by AuthorHouse 12/15/2008

ISBN: 978-1-4389-3100-5 (sc)

Library of Congress Control Number: 2008910481

Printed in the United States of America
Bloomington, Indiana

This book is printed on acid-free paper.

Front cover photo: French publicity still of Danielle Darrieux
Back cover: painting by Blake Bazel

TABLE OF CONTENTS

PREFACE		vii
CHAPTER 1	**CREATIVITY DEFINED IN** *STELLO A Session with Doctor Noir* by Alfred de Vigny	1
CHAPTER 2	**CREATIVITY DEFINED IN** LITTLE HERR FRIEDEMANN by Thomas Mann	9
CHAPTER 3	**CREATIVITY DEFINED IN** THE JOKER by Thomas Mann	11
CHAPTER 4	**CREATIVITY DEFINED IN** TRISTAN by Thomas Mann	13
CHAPTER 5	**CREATIVITY DEFINED IN** TONIO KRÖGER by Thomas Mann	15
CHAPTER 6	**CREATIVITY DEFINED IN** DEATH IN VENICE by Thomas Mann	22
CHAPTER 7	**CREATIVITY DEFINED IN** ECKBERT THE FAIR by Ludwig Tieck	26
CHAPTER 8	**CREATIVITY DEFINED IN** THE RUNEMBERG by Ludwig Tieck	28
CHAPTER 9	**CREATIVITY DEFINED IN** DON GIOVANNI by E.T.A. Hoffmann	30
CHAPTER 10	**CREATIVITY DEFINED IN** THE JESUIT CHAPEL IN G. by E.T.A. Hoffmann	32
CHAPTER 11	**CREATIVITY DEFINED IN** WOMEN IN LOVE by D.H. Lawrence	33
CHAPTER 12	**CREATIVITY DEFINED IN** FOR A NIGHT OF LOVE by Émile Zola	38
CHAPTER 13	**CREATIVITY DEFINED IN** HOTEL DU LAC by Anita Brookner	39
CHAPTER 14	**CREATIVITY DEFINED IN** A CLOSED EYE by Anita Brookner	42
CHAPTER 15	**CREATIVITY DEFINED IN** DOCTOR FAUSTUS by Thomas Mann	44
CHAPTER 16	**CREATIVITY DEFINED IN** THE FLAME by Gabriele D'Annunzio	57
CHAPTER 17	**CREATIVITY DEFINED IN** SENTIMENTAL EDUCATION by Gustave Flaubert	103

CHAPTER 18	**CREATIVITY DEFINED IN** KALLOCAIN by Karin Boye	114
CHAPTER 19	**CREATIVITY DEFINED IN** THE VIRGIN AND THE GIPSY by D.H. Lawrence	119
CHAPTER 20	**CREATIVITY DEFINED IN** THE AWAKENING by Kate Chopin	123
CHAPTER 21	**CREATIVITY DEFINED IN** SELECTED WRITINGS by Gerard de Nerval	132
CHAPTER 22	**CREATIVITY DEFINED IN** INFERNO by August Strindberg	150
CHAPTER 23	**CREATIVITY DEFINED IN** TESS OF THE D'URBERVILLES by Thomas Hardy	170
CHAPTER 24	**CREATIVITY DEFINED IN** GERTRUDE by Hermann Hesse	184
CHAPTER 25	**CREATIVITY DEFINED IN** CHRISTMAS HOLIDAY by W. Somerset Maugham	205
CHAPTER 26	**CREATIVITY DEFINED IN** THE PICTURE OF DORIAN GRAY by Oscar Wilde	213
CHAPTER 27	**CREATIVITY DEFINED IN** REQUIEM FOR A WOMAN by Rainer Maria Rilke	231

BOOKS CITED IN CREATIVITY DEFINED   234

AFTERWORD WITH MARISOL BLANCO'S POEM "ODYSSEY".   237

CREATIVITY DEFINED INDEX   242

PREFACE

The veritable tradition in great things is not to repeat what others have done, but to rediscover the spirit that created these great things—and creates utterly different things in different times.

- Paul Valéry, French poet and essayist (1871-1945)

I want to tell you that in my experience everyone is, or can be, creative in some way or another. You have to be patient and listen to your inner voice which will tell you what to do. And be prepared to take your time.

- Anita Brookner, English author and critic of literature and art, discusses creativity with the editor of *Creativity Defined*

Gene Cash, Ph.D. (2008 – 2009 President of the National Association for School Psychologists) asked me at my dissertation proposal, "What is your definition of *creativity*?" CREATIVITY DEFINED is my answer to Dr. Gene Cash's excellent question. My goal in editing this book was to come up with a thorough and objective explanation of creativity.

In CREATIVITY DEFINED, it is the great writers of the 19th and 20th century who are defining creativity and sharing their insight on ways to be more creative. This book is comprised of lines selected from 27 classic literary works. These lines will allow you to better understand the many facets of creativity. Also, they will encourage you to be more creative in your life.

The CREATIVITY DEFINED INDEX lists components of creativity and the passage numbers in this book in which they are mentioned by the renowned authors. The words that appear in the index and that are in bold print in the selected lines throughout the book are "keywords" that define creativity.

The Afterword includes a poem and drawing by Marisol Blanco.

Blake Bazel, M.S.

CHAPTER 1
STELLO A Session with Doctor Noir
by Alfred de Vigny

1.

(Doctor Noir speaking to Stello) Are you a **poet**? Examine yourself well, and tell me whether you feel within yourself that you are a poet.

Stello heaved a deep sigh, and after musing for a moment, replied, in the monotonous cadence of the evening prayer, his forehead resting on a pillow as if he would have liked to bury his whole head in it:

I have **faith** in myself because I **feel** at the bottom of my heart a **secret power**, something indefinable and invisible, which is at once a presentiment of the future and an **insight** into the past, where lie the mysterious germs of the present. I have faith in myself because there exists in creation nothing **beautiful**, nothing grand, nothing **harmonious** which does not send a prophetic quiver through me, which does not make itself felt in my very bowels, and fill my eyes with **divine** and **mysterious** tears. I believe firmly that I have been called to a **transcendental** vocation; the proof is the **boundless** pity which all men, my companions in misfortune, inspire in me, and my constant **desire**, to reach out to them and sustain them with words of sympathy and love. Like a flame that sinks and gutters when the oil that feeds it fails the wick, but **soars** in splendor and lights the temple to the very roof when the lamp is filled, so I too feel the light of thought and **inspiration** grow dim when **Love**, that indefinable force that sustains my life, leaves me forsaken of its **ardent strength**; but while it lives in me, my whole

soul lights up, and I understand at once **Eternity, Infinity**, the whole Creation, together with its creatures and its Fate; and then it is that the golden phoenix of illusion settles on my lips, and sings.

"But I believe that once the gift of fortifying the weak begins to wither in the poet, then his life will also wither; for if he is not of use to everyone, he is of no use at all."

"I believe in the **eternal struggle** of our **inner life**, which warms and fructifies, against the external life, which withers and repels, and I invoke from above the thoughts and that kindle and concentrate the poetic forces of my life; Devotion and Pity."

2.

(Chatterton speaking to Kitty Bell) There exists a tribe of men with wizened hearts and piercing eyes, armed with pincers and claws; the whole ant-heap of them march out when the most insignificant book appears, fling themselves on it, swarm over it, gnaw it, tear it, bore their way into it, riddle it through and through faster and more thoroughly than any species of bookworm. No **emotion** has ever been known to touch any member of this family, no **inspiration exalts** them, no light can rejoice or warm them; this indestructible race of executioners, with the blood of the viper or the toad in their veins, sees the spots on the sun clearly enough, but has never noticed its light; they make straight for every weakness; pullulate endlessly in the very wounds they have inflicted, in the blood and tears which they have caused; for ever biting and never bitten, sheltered from every blow by their insignificance, their baseness, their shifty tricks and their perfidious machinations.

3.

(Stello speaking to Dr. Noir) The mediocre masses make very few demands on the mediocrities of a higher order, submitting stupidly and cheerfully to their guidance.

4.

(Chatterton speaking to Beckford) The **Poet seeks** in the stars the course traced by the finger of **God.**

5.

(Dr. Noir speaking to Stello) Men everywhere have always been the same weak and simple creatures, more or less knocked about and distorted by their destiny. Only the strongest or the best of them **rebel** against it and mould it to their taste, instead of letting themselves be kneaded by its capricious hand.

6.

(Dr. Noir speaking to Chénier) **Poets** have **insight** into the future.

7.

(Stello speaking to Dr. Noir) In their anxiety to connect everything, at all costs, to a cause, a theory, a Synthesis from which everything can be derived and by which everything will be explained, I perceive a perennial weakness in men.

8.

(Stello speaking to Dr. Noir) And so, of the three forms of Power, the first is afraid of us, the second scorns us as useless, the third one hates us and tries to pull us down.

9.

(Dr. Noir speaking to Stello) The **Imagination**, in its company of the Elect, is as far superior to Judgement, with no one to show but its orators, as the Olympian **gods** are above the demi-gods. The most precious gift of heaven is also the rarest one… Do you not see that a century may give birth to three Poets, as compared with a whole crowd of very clever and able logicians and sophists? Imagination contains in itself both Judgement and Memory, and without them it could not exist. What moves men, if not emotion? What creates **emotion**, if not **art**? And who teaches men art, if not **God** Himself? For the **Poet** has no master, and all disciplines can be learned except his.—You ask me what institutions, what laws, what doctrines I have bequeathed to any state? None to any single nation, but an **eternal** one for the entire world. I belong not to a city but to the Universe. Your doctrines, your laws, your institutions, were good for a people and for an age, and they died with them; whereas the sublime works of Art stand forever as they rise, and all of them direct unhappy mankind towards the imperishable law of **Love** and Pity.

10.

(Dr. Noir speaking to Stello) The **Poet's destiny**, is nothing but the constant sense of his **mission** that every man who **feels** the **Muse** at the bottom of his heart must own.—The Muse has not come for nothing; it knows what it is about, but the Poet cannot tell its purposes beforehand. It is only in the moment of his **inspiration** that he finds out.—His mission is to **produce**, and to produce only when he hears the **secret voice**. He must wait for it. Let no foreign influence dictate his words, lest they become perishable. Let him not worry that his work may be useless; if it be **beautiful**, it will be useful by virtue of that fact alone, since it will unite men in a common reverence and contemplation of itself, and of the **idea** for which it stands.

11.

(Stello discussing with Dr. Noir) To hold power has always meant to manipulate idiots and circumstances; and these circumstances and these idiots, tossed together, bring about those coincidences to which even the greatest men confess they owe most of their fame. But to whom does the **Poet** owe his, other than to himself? The height, the depth, and the breadth of his work and of his future renown correspond exactly to the three dimensions of his brain. He exists by his own achievement; he is what he is, and his **work** is himself.

12.

(Dr. Noir speaking to Stello) **Alone** and **Free**, accomplish your **Mission**. Follow the conditions of your being, free from the influence of all Associations, no matter how attractive. For **solitude** is the only source of **inspiration**. Solitude is holy. All associations suffer from the vices of the convent. They tend to regiment and to direct intelligence, and bit by bit they lay the foundations of a tyrannical authority that deprives the mind of **liberty** and **individuality** (without which it is nothing), and seeks to stifle **genius** itself under the weight of collective jealousy. In the Assemblies, the Corporations, the Companies, the Schools, the Academies, and all that resembles them, the intriguing mediocrities gradually occupy the dominant positions by their crude busyness, and by that kind of chicanery to which great and generous **spirits** cannot stoop.

13.

(Dr. Noir speaking to Stello) The **Imagination** lives only by virtue of **spontaneous emotions peculiar** to the temperament and the idiosyncrasies of an **individual**.

14.

(Dr. Noir speaking to Stello) The **Poets** and the **Artists** are alone among men in the **pleasure** of being able to accomplish their **mission** in **solitude**. Let them enjoy the happiness of not being confounded with the crowds that gather around the least celebrity, appropriate him, enclose him, embrace him, encyst him, and finally address him as "We."

15.

(Dr. Noir speaking to Stello) Yes, the **imagination** of the **Poet** is as inconstant as that of a fifteen-year-old experiencing the first impressions of **love**. The Poet's imagination cannot be directed, because it has not been taught to him. Remove its wings and it will die.

16.

(Dr. Noir speaking to Stello) The **mission** of the **Poet** or the **Artist** is to **produce** his **works**, and all he produces is useful if it be found **beautiful**.

17.

(Dr. Noir speaking to Stello) A **Poet** gives his own measure in his **work**; the man who is attached to Power can give his measure only in the functions he performs. Fortunate is the former, unhappy the latter; for its progress occurs in their minds, the Poet can leap forward in his work; the other man must wait for the slow series of opportunities that life may provide in the gradual evolution of his career.

18.

(Dr. Noir speaking to Stello) For a man who is discouraged will often, through laziness of spirit, fall into the temptation of action and involvement in the common interest, when he sees how far beneath him it is and how easy it is to take a superior role in such activity. By so doing he abandons his own **path**, and if he leaves it often, he will lose it forever.

19.

(Dr. Noir speaking to Stello) But do not hope that a great work will be pondered over, or that any book will be read as it was conceived.

CHAPTER 2
LITTLE HERR FRIEDEMANN
by Thomas Mann

20.

(Johannes speaking) He had long been accustomed to going his own way and not sharing the interests of other people.

21.

(Johannes speaking) A **walk** in springtime through the parks outside the town, the scent of a flower, the song of a bird—surely these were things to be thankful for

---

22.

(Johannes speaking) A capacity for the enjoyment of life presupposes education, indeed that education always adds at once to that capacity, and he took pains to **educate** himself.

23.

(Johannes speaking) He came to see that there is nothing that cannot be enjoyed and that it is almost absurd to distinguish between happy and unhappy experiences. He accepted all his **sensations** and moods as they came to him, he welcomed and cultivated them, whether they were sad or glad: even his unfulfilled wishes, even his heart's **longing.** It was precious to him for its own sake, and he would tell himself that if it ever came to fulfillment the best part of the **pleasure** would be over.

CHAPTER 3
THE JOKER
by Thomas Mann

24.

(narrator speaking) One might almost suppose that a man's **inner experiences** become all the more violent and disturbing the more undisturbed and uncommitted and detached from the world his outward life is. There is no help for it: life has to be lived—and if one refuses to be a man of action and retires into the quiet of a hermit's solitude, even then the vicissitudes of existence will assault one inwardly, they will still be there to test one's character and to prove one a **hero** or a half-wit.

25.

(narrator speaking) I read a great deal, in fact I **read** everything I could lay my hands on, and I was exceedingly impressionable. I had an intuitive understanding of the personalities of authors, I seemed to see in each of them a reflection of myself, and I would go on **thinking** and **feeling** in the style of a particular book until a new one had **influenced** me in its turn. In my room, the room where I had once set up my puppet theater, I now sat with a book on my knees, looking up at the portraits of my two ancestors, savoring the inflections of the writer to whom I had surrendered myself, and with an unproductive **chaos** of half-formed thoughts and fanciful **images** filling my mind…

26.

(narrator speaking) I felt something of the **pride** of **genius**, such as a great **painter** must feel who has condescended to scribble an absurd yet brilliant caricature on the top of a table at which he is sitting among friends.

27.

(narrator speaking) There was a certain **idealistic** purposefulness in my arrangements, that I made it my serious business to ensure that each of my days should "contain" as much as possible.

28.

(narrator speaking) There is only one real misfortune: to forfeit one's own good opinion of oneself. To have lost one's **self-respect**: that is what unhappiness is.

CHAPTER 4
TRISTAN
by Thomas Mann

29.

(Herr Klöterjahn's wife speaking to Herr Spinell) It suggests something to me that I partly understand, a certain **feeling** of **independence** and **freedom**, even a certain disrespect for reality—although I know that reality is more deserving of respect than anything else, indeed that it is the only truly respectable thing… And then I realize that there is something beyond what we can see and touch, something more delicate…

30.

(narrator speaking about Herr Spinell) In yellowish twilight he was sitting bowed over the desk and **writing**—he was writing one of those numerous letters which he sent to the post every week and to which, comically enough, he usually received no reply.

31.

(Herr Spinell writing) "Sir!" he had written, "I am addressing the following lines to you because I simply cannot help it—because my heart is so full of what I have to say to you that it aches and trembles, and the words come to me in such a rush that they would choke me if I could not unburden myself of them in this letter…"

32.

(Herr Spinell writing) "I am," the letter continued, "under an inescapable compulsion to make you see what I see, to make you share the inextinguishable **vision** that has haunted me for weeks, to make you see it with my eyes, illuminated by the language in which I myself would express what I inwardly behold. An imperative **instinct** bids me communicate my experiences to the world, to communicate them in unforgettable words each chosen and placed with burning accuracy; and this is an instinct which it is my habit to obey."

33.

(Herr Spinell writing) "Do you remember this scene, sir? Did you even see it? No, you did not. It was not for your eyes, and yours were not the ears to hear the chaste sweetness of that melody. Had you seen it, you would not have dared to draw breath, and your heart would have checked its beat. You would have had to withdraw, go back into life, back to your own life, and preserve what you had beheld as something untouchable and inviolable, as a sacred treasure within your **soul**, to the end of your earthly days."

CHAPTER 5
TONIO KRÖGER
by Thomas Mann

34.

(narrator speaking of Tonio) ... life had already imparted this hard and simple **truth** to his fourteen-year-old **soul**; and his nature was such that when he learned something in this way he took careful note of it, inwardly **writing** it down, so to speak, and even taking a certain **pleasure** in it—though without, of course, modifying his own behavior in the light of it or turning it to any practical account. He had, moreover, the kind of mind that found such lessons much more important and interesting than any of the knowledge that was forced on him at school; indeed, as he sat through the hours of instruction in the vaulted Gothic classrooms, he would chiefly be occupied in savoring these **insights** to their very depths and **thinking** out all their implications. And this pastime would give his just the same sort of satisfaction as he felt when he **wandered** round his own room with his violin (for he played the violin) and drew from it notes of such tenderness as only he could draw, notes which he mingled with the rippling sound of the fountain down in the garden as it leaped and **danced** under the branches of the old walnut tree.

35.

(narrator speaking of Tonio) The fountain, the old walnut tree, his violin and the **sea** in the distance, The Baltic Sea to whose summer reveries he could **listen** when he visited in the holidays, these were the things he **loved**, the things which, so to speak, he arranged around himself and among which his **inner life** evolved—things with names that may be employed to **poetry** in good effect, and which did indeed very frequently recur in the poems that Tonio Kröger from time to time composed.

36.

(narrator speaking of Tonio) And occasionally he would **reflect**: "But why am I **peculiar**, why do I fight against everything, why am I in the masters' bad books and a **stranger** among the other boys? Just look at them, the good pupils and the solid mediocre ones! They don't find the masters ridiculous, they don't **write poetry** and they only think the kind of thoughts that one does and should think, the kind that can be spoken aloud. How decent they must feel, how at peace with everything and everyone! It must be good to be like that... But what is the matter with me, and what will come of it all?"

37.

(Tonio reflecting) Had she laughed at him too, like all the others? Yes, she had, however much he would have liked to deny it for her sake and his. And yet he had only joined in the *moulinet des dames* because he had been so engrossed by her presence. And what did it matter anyway?

One day perhaps they would stop laughing. Had he not recently had a **poem** accepted by a periodical—even if the periodical had gone out of business before the poem could appear? The day was coming when he would be famous and when everything he **wrote** would be printed; and then it would be seen whether that would not impress Inge Holm.

38.

(Tonio reflecting) For happiness, he told himself, does not consist in being loved; that merely gratifies one's vanity and is mingled with repugnance. Happiness consists in **loving**—and perhaps snatching a few little moments of illusory nearness to the beloved. And he inwardly noted down this **reflection**, thought out all its implications and savored it to its very depths.

39.

(narrator speaking of Tonio) He surrendered himself utterly to that power which he felt to be the sublimest power on earth, to the service of which he felt called and which promised him honor and renown: the **power** of **intellect** and words, a power that sits smilingly enthroned above mere inarticulate, unconscious life. He surrendered to it with **youthful passion**, and it rewarded him with all that it has to give, while inexorably exacting its full price in return.

It sharpened his perceptions and enabled him to see through the high-sounding phrases that swell the human breast, it unlocked for him the **mysteries** of the human mind and of his own, it made him clear-sighted, it showed him life from the inside and revealed to him the fundamental motives behind what men say and do.

40.

(narrator speaking of Tonio) He worked, not like a man who works in order to live, but like one who has no **desire** but to **work**, because he sets no store by himself as a living human being, seeks recognition only as a creative **artist**, and spends the rest of his time in a gray incognito, like an actor with his makeup off, who has no identity when he is not performing. He worked in **silence**, in invisible **privacy**, for he utterly despised those minor hacks who treated their talent as a social ornament…

41.

(Tonio speaking to Lisaveta) "I've just been **working**, Lisaveta, and inside my head everything looks just as it does on this canvass. A skeleton, a faint sketch, a mess of corrections, and a few patches of color, to be sure; and now I come here and see the same thing. And the same **contradiction** is here too," he said, sniffing the air, "the same conflict that was bothering me at home. It's odd. Once a thought has got hold of you, you find **expressions** of it everywhere, you even smell it in the wind."

42.

(Tonio speaking to Lisaveta) "Using his admiration for my **genius** as an enrichment and a **stimulus**."

43.

(Tonio speaking to Lisaveta) "A real **artist** is not one who has taken up art as his profession, but a man predestined and foredoomed to it; and such an artist can be picked out from a crowd by anyone with the slightest perspicacity. You can read in his face that he is a man apart, a man who does not belong, who feels that he is recognized and is being watched; there is somehow an air of royalty about him and at the same time an air of embarrassment. A prince walking incognito among the people wears a rather similar expression. But the incognito doesn't work."

44.

(Tonio speaking to Lisaveta) "But what *is* an **artist**? I know of no other question to which human complacency and incuriosity have remained so impervious. 'That sort of thing is a gift,' say average decent folk humbly, when a work of art has produced its intended effect upon them; and because of the goodness in their hearts they assume that exhilarating and noble effects must necessarily have exhilarating and noble causes, it never enters their heads that the origins of this so-called 'gift' may well be extremely dubious and extremely disreputable."

45.

(Tonio speaking to Lisaveta) "No one, my dear, has a right to call himself an **artist** if his profoundest craving is for the refined, the eccentric and the satanic—if his heart knows no **longing** for **innocence**, **simplicity** and living **warmth**, for a little friendship and self-surrender and familiarity and human happiness."

46.

(Tonio thinking to himself) To **long** to be able to live simply for one's **feelings** alone, to rest **idly** in sweet self-sufficient **emotion**, uncompelled to translate it into activity, unconstrained to dance—and to have to **dance** nevertheless, to have to be alert and nimble and perform the **difficult**, difficult and perilous sword-dance of **art**, and never to be able quite to forget the humiliating paradox of having to dance when one's heart is heavy with **love**.

47.

(Tonio speaking to Lisaveta) "What I have achieved so far is nothing, not much, as good as nothing. I shall **improve** on it, Lisaveta—this I promise you. As I write this, I can hear below me the roar of the **sea**, and I close my eyes. I gaze into an **unborn**, unembodied world that demands to be ordered and shaped, I see before me a host of shadowy human figures whose gestures implore me to cast upon them the spell that shall be their deliverance: tragic and comic figures, and some that are both at once—and to these I am strongly drawn. But my **deepest** and most **secret love** belongs to the fair-haired and the blue-eyed, the bright **children** of life, the happy, the charming and the ordinary.

Do not disparage this love, Lisaveta; it is good and fruitful. In it there is **longing**, and sad envy, and just a touch of contempt, and a whole world of **innocent delight**."

CHAPTER 6
DEATH IN VENICE
by Thomas Mann

48.

(narrator speaking about Gustav Aschenbach) Too preoccupied with the tasks imposed upon him by his own **sensibility** and by the collective European psyche, too heavily burdened with the compulsion to **produce**, too shy of distraction to have learned how to take leisure and pleasure in the colorful external world, he had been perfectly well satisfied to have no more detailed a view of the earth's surface than anyone can acquire without stirring far from home, and he had never even been tempted to venture outside Europe. This had been more especially the case since his life had begun its gradual decline and his **artist's** fear of not finishing his task—the apprehension that his time might run out before he had given the whole of himself by doing what he had it in him to do—was no longer something he could simply dismiss as an idle fancy.

49.

(narrator speaking about Gustav Aschenbach) [He took] a **walk** of same length by himself. The morning's **writing** had **overstimulated** him: his **work** had now reached a **difficult** and dangerous point which demanded the utmost care and circumspection, the most insistent and precise **effort** of **will**, and the **productive** mechanism in his mind."

50.

(narrator speaking) The observations and encounters of a devotee of **solitude** and **silence** are at once less distinct and more **penetrating** than those of the sociable man; his thoughts are weightier, **stranger**, and never without a tinge of **sadness**. **Images** and perceptions which might otherwise be easily dispelled by a glance, a laugh, an exchange of comments concern him unduly, they sink into mute depths, take on significance, become experiences**, adventures, emotions**. The fruit of solitude is **originality**, something **daringly** and **disconcertingly beautiful**, the **poetic** creation. But the fruit of solitude can also be the perverse, the disproportionate, the absurd and the forbidden.

51.

(narrator speaking of Gustav Aschenbach) There were profound reasons for his attachment to the **sea**: he **loved** it because as a **hard-working artist** he needed **rest**, needed to **escape** from the demanding complexity of phenomena and lie hidden on the bosom of the simple and the tremendous; because of a forbidden longing **deep** within him that ran quite contrary to his life's task and was for that very reason seductive, a **longing** for the unarticulated and immeasurable, for **eternity**, for nothingness. To rest in the arms of perfection is the **desire** of any man intent upon creating excellence; and is not nothingness a form of perfection?

52.

(narrator speaking of Gustav Aschenbach) His eyes embraced that noble figure at the blue water's edge, and in rising **ecstasy** he felt he was gazing on **Beauty** itself, on Form as a thought of **God**, on the one and pure perfection which dwells in the spirit and of which a human image and likeness has here been lightly and graciously set up for him to worship. Such was his **emotional** intoxication; and the aging **artist** welcomed it unhesitatingly, even greedily.

53.

(narrator speaking of Gustav Aschenbach) The **writer's joy** is the thought that can become emotion, the e**motion** that can wholly become a thought. At that time the **solitary** Aschenbach took possession and control of just such a pulsating thought, just such a precise emotion: namely, that **Nature** trembles with **rapture** when the spirit bows in homage before **Beauty**. He suddenly **desire**d to write. Eros indeed, we are told, loves **idleness** and is **born** only for the idle. But at this point of Aschenbach's crisis and visitation, his **excitement** was driving him to **produce**.

54.

(narrator speaking of Gustav Aschenbach) Aschenbach habitually let the achievements and successes of his life remind him of his ancestors, for in **imagination** he could then feel sure of their approval, of their satisfaction, of the respect they could not have withheld. And he thought of them even here and now, entangled as he was in so impermissible an experience, involved in such exotic extravagances of **feeling**; he thought, with a sad smile, of their dignified austerity, their decent manliness of character. What would they say? But for that matter, what would they have said about his entire life, a life that had **deviated** from theirs to the point of degeneracy, this life of his in compulsive service of **art,** this life about which he himself, adopting the civic values of his forefathers, had once let fall such mocking observations—and which nevertheless had essentially been so much like theirs! He too had served, he too had been a soldier and a warrior, like many of them: for art was a war, an exhausting **struggle**, it was hard these days to remain fit for it for long. A life of self-conquest and of **defiant resolve**, an astringent, steadfast and frugal life which he had turned into the symbol of that **heroism** for delicate constitutions, that heroism so much in keeping with the times—surely he might call this manly, might call it **courageous?**

55.

(Gustav Aschenbach speaking) "**Beauty** is at one and the same time **divine** and visible, and so it is indeed the **sensuous lover's path**, little Phaedrus, it is the **artist's** path to the **spirit**… for it is **passion** that **exalts** us, and the **longing** of our **soul** must remain the longing of a lover—that is our **joy** and our shame.

CHAPTER 7
ECKBERT THE FAIR
by Ludwig Tieck

56.

(narrator speaking of Eckbert and his wife) He lived a quiet, secluded life and never became involved in the feuds between his neighbors; indeed, he was rarely seen outside the walls of his own little demesne. His wife enjoyed their **solitude** as much as he, and they seemed to be very fond of each other.

57.

(Eckbert's wife speaking)   O Nature fair
*Thy **beauty** rare*
Beyond compare,
Pervades the air.
I rest in thy care,
*O **Nature** fair.*

58.

(Eckbert's wife speaking) Of an evening which she would teach me to **read**, which I quickly learned to do, and this later became and endless source of **delight** to me in my **solitude**.

59.

(Eckbert's wife speaking) It is a tragedy that man has been given his **intelligence** only in order that he may destroy the **innocence** of his own **soul**.

CHAPTER 8
THE RUNEMBERG
by Ludwig Tieck

60.

(Narrator speaking of Christian) In the depths of the mountains a young gamekeeper sat in **pensive solitude** among the birds. Only the rustling of the trees and the murmur of the streams broke the **silence**. He **reflected** on his fate: though still very young, he had already left his father and mother, the familiar surroundings of home and all of his friends in the village to get away from the monotony of the daily round and find a **new** world.

61.

(The stranger speaking to Christian) 'Anyone who knows how to look,' rejoined the stranger, 'and whose heart is really in the **search**, is bound to find old friends there and ancient glories—indeed, all the things for which one most **deeply longs**.'

62.

(Narrator speaking of Christian) **Driven** on by fantastic **visions** and inexplicable **desires**, he paid no heed to the yawning depths below that threatened to devour him.

63.

(Narrator speaking of Christian) A **vision** of **harmony** and of **beautiful** figures, of **ecstasies** and **longings** appeared before him, a flood of glorious melodies, some lighthearted, some sad, filled his head and he was moved to the depths of his **soul**. A world of **suffering** and **hope** opened up before him, a world where wholehearted trust and **proud confidence** reigned and where great rivers wended their lonesome way down to the **sea**. He felt a completely **different** person.

64.

(Christian speaking to his father) 'For months, even years, I am able to forget my **spiritual** condition and live a double life, as it were, with the greatest of ease. Then the **power** of my **true self** rises like a **new** moon and overcomes the hostile power within me. I could have been happy and contented but one strange night a **mysterious** sign was branded on my **soul**; mostly this magic symbol lies dormant and seems to have disappeared altogether but then it flares up like a festering wound and spreads everywhere. It takes hold of my thoughts and **feelings, transforms** and swallows up everything around me. As a madman is horrified by the sight of water and the poison within him becomes more virulent, so all these jagged shapes, all these lines and rays of light seek to release the creature within me and I am seized with fear. And as this fear invades my mind from without, so I fight, tortured and **tormented**, to drive it out again, back to the world from whence it came, and regain my composure.'

CHAPTER 9
DON GIOVANNI
by E.T.A. Hoffmann

65.

(Hoffmann speaking about viewing an opera) I had been so happy in the box **alone,** enjoying the performance of this great masterpiece without disturbance, sending out my **emotional** feelers, as it were, and drawing it towards me as though with the tentacles of an octopus. One thoughtless word could have violently destroyed the sense of **exultation** which I was reveling in the glories of the **poetry** and the **music.** I therefore decided to ignore the intruder and devote myself entirely to the **work**, disdaining to spare him a glance or a word.

66.

(Hoffmann speaking of Donna Anna) **Music** had been her whole life, she said, and she felt that she grasped through song the **meaning** of a **mysterious**, **deep**-seated reality which could not be expressed in words.

67.

(Donna Anna speaking to Hoffmann) Your **spirit** opened itself to me in song and I understood you—'it was of you I was singing, and your melodies were *me*!'

68.

(Hoffmann observing about himself) It was as though my most wonderful **dreams** in another world were now becoming part of real life, the **secret** pining of my **ecstatic spirit** captured in the sounds of the **music** and issuing in a miraculous **revelation**.

CHAPTER 10
THE JESUIT CHAPEL IN G.
by E.T.A. Hoffmann

69.

(Maltese painter speaking to Berthold) The **spirit** that issued from the **work** as a whole wafted you into a higher realm.

70.

(Berthold's thoughts to himself after listening to the Maltese painter) **A voice** within him cried: 'No! Stop all these frantic efforts! They are like those of a blind man groping his uncertain way past false obstacles. Away with everything that has dazzled and misled me up to now!'

71.

(Florentin speaking to Berthold) It is my view that one should **strengthen** oneself through direct contact with organic **nature** so as to find one's way into the **deeper** realm of **mystery**.

CHAPTER 11
WOMEN IN LOVE
by D.H. Lawrence

72.

(narrator speaking of Ursula) She lived a good deal by herself, to herself, working, passing, on from day to day, and always **thinking**, trying to lay hold on life, to grasp it in her own understanding.

73.

(narrator speaking of Gudrun) There was a certain **playfulness** about her too.

74.

(Birkin speaking) You've got to lapse out before you can know what **sensual** reality is, lapse into unknowingness, and give up your volition. You've got to do it. You've got to learn not-to-be, before you can come into being.

75.

(Birkin speaking) You've got very badly to want to get rid of the old before anything **new** will appear—even in the self.

76.

(Halliday speaking) Oh—one would *feel* things instead of merely looking at them. I should **feel** the air move against me, and feel the things I touched, instead of having only to look at them.

77.

(Hermione speaking) To me the **pleasure** of knowing is so great, so *wonderful*—nothing has meant so much to me in all life, as certain **knowledge**.

78.

(Birkin speaking) He preferred his own madness, to the regular sanity. He rejoiced in his own madness, he was **free**. He did not want that old sanity of the world, which was become so repulsive. He rejoiced in the **new-found** world of his madness. It was so fresh and delicate and so satisfying.

79.

(Ursula speaking to Birkin) Just be oneself, like a walking flower.

80.

(Hermione speaking) If only we could learn how to use our **will**, we could do anything. The will can cure anything, and put anything right.

81.

(narrator speaking of Ursula) She could not consider anymore, what anybody would say of her or think about her. People had passed out of her range, she was absolved. She had fallen **strange** and dim, out of the sheath of the material life, as a berry falls from the only world it has ever known, down out of the sheath on to the real **unknown**…

To live mechanized and cut off within the motion of the **will**, to live as an entity absolved from the **unknown**, that is shameful and ignominious.

82.

(narrator speaking of Birkin) Best of all to **persist** and persist, and persist forever, till one were satisfied in life.

83.

(Birkin speaking to Gerald) For special natures you must give a special world... Instead of chopping yourself down to fit the world, chop the world down to fit yourself. As a matter of fact, two exceptional people make another world. Do you *want* to be normal or ordinary? It's a lie. You want to be **free** and extraordinary, in an extraordinary world of **liberty**...

Artists produce for each other the world that is fit to live in.

84.

(narrator speaking of Gudrun) She had an insatiable **curiosity** to see and to know everything.

85.

(Birkin's thoughts) The reality of **beauty**, the reality of happiness in warm creation.

86.

(Ursula speaking to Birkin) You always seem to think you can *force* the flowers to come out. People must **love** us because they love us—you can't *make* them... You must learn to be **alone**.

87.

(narrator speaking about Ursula) She was glad in **hope**, glorious and **free,** full of life and **liberty.**

88.

(Ursula speaking to Gudrun) One can see it through in one's **soul,** long enough before it sees itself through in actuality. And then, when one has seen one's soul, one is something else…

I believe what we must fulfill comes out of the **unknown** to us.

89.

(narrator speaking about Gerald) He talked to her, continued the discussions of **art,** of life, in which they both found such **pleasure.**

90.

(narrator speaking of Gerald and Gudrun) To live again the lives of the great **artists.**

91.

(Gudrun speaking) **Escape** so much hideous boring repetition.

CHAPTER 12
FOR A NIGHT OF LOVE
by Émile Zola

92.

(narrator speaking of Julien) Julien's **paradise**, the one place where he breathed **freely**, was his room.

93.

(narrator speaking of Julien) His only **passion** was **music**.

94.

(narrator speaking of Julien) Julien had **learned** by himself to play the flute.

95.

(narrator speaking of Julien) He grew **bold** enough to get the flute.

CHAPTER 13
HOTEL DU LAC
by Anita Brookner

96.

(narrator speaking of Edith) The **silence** engulfed her once she was past the town's one intersection, and it seemed as if she might walk for ever, uninterrupted, with only her thoughts for company.

97.

(narrator speaking of Edith) As if she must pursue this **path** until its purpose were revealed to her.

98.

(narrator speaking of Edith) She wanted to be **alone**, in her room, so as to **think**.

99.

(narrator speaking of Edith) She pulled out her papers, re-read her last paragraph, and bent her head obediently to her daily task of **fantasy**.

Blake Bazel, M.S.

100.

(narrator speaking of Edith) a **dreaming,** glowing **idleness, inspired** by Delacroix

---

101.

(Mr. Neville speaking to Edith) 'It is a great mistake,' he resumed, after a pause, 'to confuse happiness with one particular situation, one particular person. Since I **freed** myself from all of that I have **discovered** the **secret** of contentment.'

102.

(Mr. Neville speaking to Edith) 'If one is prepared to do the one thing one is drilled out of doing from earliest childhood—simply please oneself—there is no reason why one should ever be unhappy again.'

103.

(Mr. Neville speaking to Edith) 'It is the simplest thing in the world to decide what you want to do— or, rather, what you don't want to do— and just to act on that.'

104.

(Mr. Neville speaking to Edith) 'You must learn to discount the others." Within your own scope you can accomplish much more. You can be self-centered, and that is a marvelous lesson to **learn**. To assume your own centrality may mean an entirely **new** life.'

105.

(Mr. Neville speaking to Edith) 'You cannot live someone else's life. You can only live your own.'

106.

(narrator speaking of Edith) She might please herself, simply by **wishing** it so.

107.

(narrator speaking of Edith) She **longed** for such **solitude**, like a **child** who has become overexcited at a party, and who should have been taken home, by a prudent nurse, some time ago.

108.

(narrator speaking of Edith) **Hopes** and **wishes** are what should be proclaimed, most strenuously proclaimed, if anyone is to be jolted into the necessity of taking note of them, let alone an obligation to fulfill them.

CHAPTER 14
A CLOSED EYE
by Anita Brookner

109.

(Harriet writing to Lizzie) I have had a great deal of time since then in which to **reflect**, and although I have reached no very firm conclusions, I do know what **courage** is needed to see one through a life.

110.

(narrator speaking of Monsieur Papineau) A man of serenity, naïve, **hopeful**, **childlike**, he relished what the day brought him as only the very **innocent** can afford to do.

111.

(narrator speaking of Harriet) In the half doze of early afternoon, she disposed of her present life, and substituted for it the life of the **imagination**.

112.

(narrator speaking of Harriet) She simply knew that for once she was acting on her own volition, and the **sensation** was almost fulfillment in itself.

113.

(narrator speaking of Harriet) She knew that she had a choice, and to deny that choice, or the possibility of choice, would be fatal.

114.

(narrator speaking of Harriet) With this sudden **daring** [she] would **rediscover** her marvelous **solitude**.

115.

(narrator speaking of Harriet) Yet she could see that somehow her own unconsummated **longings** had derived an odd **beauty** from the very fact of being unconsummated. In whatever **dreams** and **desires** that she had entertained she had always seen herself as **free** and unencumbered.

CHAPTER 15
DOCTOR FAUSTUS
by Thomas Mann

116.

(Zeitblom speaking) A **lively** and **loving** eye for man's **beauty**.

117.

(Zeitblom speaking) [I am] **devoted** to it [music] with all my heart.

118.

(narrator speaking of Leverkühn) For although his whole life long the **artist** may remain nearer, if not to say, more **faithful** to his childhood than the man who specializes in practical reality, although one can say that, unlike the latter, he abides in the **dreamlike,** purely human, and **playful** state of the **child**, nevertheless the artist's **journey** from those pristine early years to the late, unforeseen stages of his development is endlessly longer, **wilder, stranger**—and more disturbing for those who watch—than that of the everyday person, for whom the thought that he, too, was once a child is cause for not half so many tears.

119.

(narrator speaking) Beethoven had been far more subjective, if not to say, far more "personal,"... he had been much more intent on letting all conventions, formulas, and flourishes (of which music was full after all) be consumed by personal **expression**, on fusing all that with the subjective dynamic.

120.

(narrator speaking) Beissel had never enjoyed an education worth the name, but once **awakened**, he had taught himself to master **reading** and writing; and since his heart surged with mystical **feelings** and **ideas**, he came to exercise his leadership primarily as a **writer** and **poet**.

121.

(narrator speaking) He set about to **work** out his own **music** theory.

122.

(narrator speaking) He wanted to begin **anew**, do things better.

123.

(narrator speaking) He had at the same time brought Adrian into first contact with the greatest things, opening for him the realm of world literature, **awakening** his **curiosity** with presentations that lured him into the vast expanses of the Russian, English, and French novel.

124.

(narrator speaking of Leverkühn) Digressing and combining, he went from one thing to a thousand others, first because he had endless things in his head and one thought **inspired** another, but more especially because he had a **passion** for comparing, **discovering** relationships, proving influences, laying bare the interwoven connections of culture.

125.

(Leverkühn speaking) It [greatness] is a test of **courage**.

126.

(narrator speaking) the highest and loftiest sphere of **knowledge**, the summit of thought, is achieved, supplying the **inspired intellect** with its most sublime **goal**.

127.

(Leverkühn speaking) Strange, how people always want to tug you down their own path. You can't please everyone.

128.

(narrator speaking) For is not that fledgling moment of dawning **freedom**, when the school door closes behind us, when the shell of the town in which we have grown up cracks open, and the world lies before us—is that moment not the happiest or at least the most excitingly expectant in all our lives?

129.

(narrator speaking) One is **free** to **strive**, to survey the world with fresh **senses** and gather in its harvest.

130.

(narrator speaking) **Freedom** is a very great thing, the prerequisite of creation…

131.

(narrator speaking about Deutschlin) Human creativity's having been regarded as coming from on high—as a distant reflection of the **power** of **divine** being, as an echo of the **almighty s**ummons into existence—and **productive imagination**'s having been given theological recognition after all.

132.

(Deutschlin speaking) To be **young** means to be primordial, to have remained close to the wellspring of life, means being able to rise up and shake off the fetters of an outmoded civilization

133.

(Deutschlin speaking) … to **dare** what others lack the vital **courage** to do—to plunge back into what is elemental. The courage of youth— that is the spirit of dying and becoming, the **knowledge** of **death** and rebirth.

134.

(Deutschlin speaking) It is the directness**,** the **courage**, and the depth of one's personal life, the **will** and ability to experience and live out in its full vitality.

135.

(Leverkühn speaking) I am playing a lot of Chopin and **reading** about him. I **love** what is angelic in his figure, recalling Shelley, his **eccentrically** and **mysteriously** veiled… his rebuff to material experience.

136.

(narrator speaking of Leverkühn) Teacher and pupil were essentially quite far apart in matters of **musical instinct** and intent—indeed, any aspirant in the **arts** finds himself almost by necessity dependent on the guidance of a master of his craft for whom he is already half-estranged by a generation's difference. Things only go well if the master nevertheless surmises and understands these hidden tendencies—sees them ironically, if need be—but is careful not to stand in the way of their **development**.

137.

(narrator speaking) There is an almost unresolvable conflict between the inhibitions and the **productive drives born** with **genius**, between chastity and **passion**—and the conflict is itself the naiveté from which such an **artistic** existence lives, the soil for its own arduously characteristic growth; and the unconscious **striving** to create for one's **"talent,"** for one's productive **impulse**, the scant but necessary advantage over the restraints of mockery, of arrogance of **intellectual** self-consciousness—that **instinctive** striving surely begins to stir and become determinative at the moment when the purely mechanical studies preparatory to creating art first begin to mingle with one's own **efforts** (even if still quite preliminarily and preparatory) at giving shape to one's art.

138.

(narrator speaking of Leverkühn) Let the **poem**, so its creator enjoins upon it, ask people to perceive its beauty if not is profundity. "Behold at least how **beautiful** I am!"

139.

(narrator speaking of Leverkühn) **Artistic thought**, he suggested, formed an **intellectual** category unique to itself.

140.

(narrator speaking of Rüdiger) For he felt himself **born** to be a **productive writer**... He wanted to be a **poet**, was convinced that he was one...

141.

(Leverkühn speaking of Brahms) With him, **music** disposes of all conventional flourishes, formulas, and tags and in each moment, so to speak, creates the unity of the work **anew**, out of **freedom**.

142.

(Leverkühn speaking) Engage in undisturbed conversation with my life, my fate.

143.

(narrator speaking) These **artists** pay little attention to an encircling present that bears no direct relation to the world of **work** in which they live.

144.

(Leverkühn speaking) Admire, praise, and **exalt** the **work [of the genius],** carry it away with them, refashion it among themselves, bequeath it to the culture…

145.

(Leverkühn speaking) It is not merely that you will break through the laming **difficulties** of the age—you will break through the age itself, the cultural epoch, which is to say, the epoch of this culture and its cult…

146.

(Leverkühn speaking) He could not express, he wrote its composer, how the **work** took his breath away in its **boldness**, its **novelty**.

147.

(narrator speaking) The "modern," with what was **free** and more than free, **rebellious**, as well as with passages that scorned every restraint of musical key.

148.

(Rudi speaking to Leverkühn) You can throw all the conventions overboard…

149.

(narrator speaking) [The period of creativity] in its own way was a time of **obsession**, of **painful urgency** and **distress**…

150.

(narrator speaking) [He] had been able to surrender himself **individually** to the **powers** of his own **imagination**.

151.

(Fitelberg speaking to Leverkühn) The reason is that, from childhood on, I have **striven** for higher things… —and above all for what is **new**…

152.

(narrator speaking) In the way it grabs one by the head and shoulders, it is one of those manifestations of **beauty** that border on the "**heavenly**"...

153.

(Leverkühn speaking) I am... an **interesting** loner.

154.

(Leverkühn speaking) What has existed before [may be] new after all, **new** to life so to speak, **original** and **unique**.

155.

(narrator speaking) If... every **path** to a right **goal** is right every step of the way, then one must admit that the path... was doomed at every point, at every turn, however bitter **love** may find it to endorse this logic.

156.

(narrator speaking) "earth in her winter rest" in whose womb life **secretly** continues its **work** in preparation for sprouting **anew**…"

157.

(narrator speaking) the stormy surge of **yearning**…

158.

(narrator speaking) And if I were to summarize my impression, it is as if one were lured from a solid and familiar point of departure into ever more remote regions—everything turns out **differently** from what one expected.

159.

(narrator speaking) one **new idea** follows another…

160.

(Leverkühn speaking) "I **learned** that to set limits is to go beyond them."

161.

(narrator speaking of Leverkühn) His creativity was shaped by his **intellect**.

162.

(narrator speaking of Leverkühn and then Leverkühn speaking) It was an exuberant interweaving of **inventions**, **challenges**, attainments, and summons from old tasks to the mastery of **new** ones, a **tumult** of problems that burst upon you together with their **solutions**—"A night," Adrian said, "that never grows dark for the lightning."

163.

(narrator speaking) the reconstruction of **expression**... an expressive cry of the **soul**... the heartfelt unbosoming of the [person]

164.

(narrator speaking) the sound of the human voice returned as a sound of **nature**, revealed as a sound of nature... to man, her attempt to proclaim his **solitude**.

165.

(narrator speaking) An **expressive** work, a **work** of expression, and as such is a work of **liberation**... the process by which strictest constraint is reversed into the free language of **emotion**, by which **freedom** is **born** out of constraint. He [Leverkühn] allowed me to perceive the "magic square" of a style or technique that develops the utmost variety out of materials that are always identical, a style in which there is nothing that is not thematic, nothing that could not qualify as a variation of something forever the same.

166.

(narrator speaking) A **spirit** that has **boldly** and **defiantly emancipated** itself from its origins...

CHAPTER 16
THE FLAME
by Gabriele D'Annunzio

167.

(Foscarina speaking to Stelio) what **soul** could shut out the **dreams** that you so **love** to summon up with words

---

168.

(narrator speaking of Stelio) **desire** to **transcend** the narrowness of [the]ordinary

---

169.

(Perdita speaking to Stelio) You have such **strength** and fire in you

---

170.

(narrator speaking of Stelio) [The poet felt] a sense of **intellectual joy** run through him as he saw his **imaginings** taking shape around him

---

171.

(Foscarina speaking to Stelio) You could never be lost, Stelio. You are always so sure of yourself. You hold your **destiny** in your own hands.

172.

(narrator speaking of Foscarina's reaction to Stelio) While she was not given to living at such a pitch of **intensity** without tremendous **effort**, she saw that he could sustain it as easily as if it were his natural way of life, and that he could rejoice in the miraculous world that he was constantly **renewing** through continuous creativity.

173.

(narrator speaking of Stelio) He had reached the point himself of being able to combine **art** and life intimately together.

174.

(narrator speaking of Stelio) He had reached the point of being able to **renew** ceaselessly in his own **spirit** that **mysterious** state that results in the birth of **works** of great **beauty**, and he was able to **transform** all the fleeting characters of his own existence miraculously into **ideal** figures.

175.

(narrator speaking of Stelio) He had an extraordinary gift with words, and was able to translate instantly even the most **complex** aspects of his own **sensitivity** into his **own language**

176.

(narrator speaking of Stelio) But since his **sensitivity** was as great as his **intellect**, those who loved him and were close to him were easily able to catch the **warmth** of his **passion** and enthusiasm.

177.

(narrator speaking of Stelio) They knew the extent of his ability to **feel** and to **dream**, and they knew that out of that combination flowed the **beautiful images** into which he habitually **transformed** the substance of his own **inner life**.

178.

(Perdita speaking to Stelio) beside you in that meadow—there will come into your **immortal** eyes…

179.

(Stelio speaking to Perdita) I mean that just as some people believe they are under the influence of a particular star, so we might be able to create some **ideal** correspondence between our own **souls** and some other earthly thing. Then that thing might gradually become steeped in our **essences** and become so huge in our minds that it might seem like the symbol of our very **destiny** and take on **mysterious** qualities at certain times in our lives. That's the **secret** of restoring some sense of primordial **energy** to our somewhat stultified souls. I know from experience how great a benefit we can derive from **intense** communication with some earthly thing. We have to **transform** our souls into something other, so as to feel the vital energy of the living tree flowing through our veins, as wood-nymphs do.

180.

(Stelio speaking to Perdita) So you see, for you and those few who really do **love** me, I have truly brought an ancient myth to life again by turning myself in some profound, **meaningful** way into an aspect of **eternal nature**… (may Nature grant me fully to realize myself through my **work** before I die!)

181.

(Stelio speaking to Perdita) my **talents** in accordance with the **genius**

182.

(Stelio speaking to Perdita) my **desire** for a richer, more **ardent** life

---

183.

(Stelio speaking to Perdita) my **strength** will grow according to **nature**'s plan and will lead to the result that is my **destiny**.

184.

(Stelio speaking to Perdita) There is no discord between my life and my **work**.

185.

(Stelio speaking to Perdita) how easy it is for fate to help one's **imagination** in giving a certain

---

186.

(Stelio speaking to Perdita) I believe every **intelligent** man can create his own happy ending in life, today or at any other time. All one has to do is to look at the whole confused maelstrom of life with the same sense of the fantastical that Leonardo advised his disciples to use when he told them to look at stained walls or at ashes in the fireplace, or to look at clouds or mud in other places in **search** of "miraculous **inventions**" and "**infinite** things".

187.

(Stelio speaking to Perdita) I am always finding occasion to marvel at the ease and the grace with which fate helps my **imagination** to create in **harmony**.

188.

(Stelio speaking to Perdita) I heard someone praising me. Francesco de Lizo was talking about me, and said that it was a pity such a magnificently **sensual**, princely **writer** (those were his words] should have to live in isolation, away from the stupid, uncaring throng, and celebrate the feast of "sounds, colours, and shapes" in the palace of his own **solitary dreaming**.

189.

(Donna Orsetta Contarini speaking near Stelio) There is nothing I like so much as the clear, **strong expression** of **desire**.

190.

(narrator speaking of Perdita) She allowed herself to be carried away by the **free**, elegant game he was playing, in which he always seemed to be trying out the quickness of his mind and the ease with which he could create **images**. There was something fluid in him, something voluble and **powerful** that stirred in her the twofold image of fire and of water.

191.

(Stelio speaking to Perdita) I must really be true to those **talents** that **nature** has given to me.

192.

(Stelio speaking to Perdita) I am so tempted by taking **risks**.

193.

(Stelio speaking to Perdita) I shall **improvise** it all…

194.

(Stelio speaking to Perdita) At that time my **idea** still hadn't reached the right level of **intensity** for it to become a work of **art**, and I **instinctively** gave up trying to make it cohere. But no seed is ever really lost in an active mind which is like fertile soil, and now it is coming back to me at just the right moment demanding to be heard. What **mysterious**, fair-minded fates govern the world of the mind! I had to be able to respect the first seed in order now to feel it growing and **developing** in me.

195.

(narrator speaking of Stelio) the rapid succession of different **images** that flashed across his **soul** like lightening. He was trying to **work** out the main lines that would shape his **new** work. He was so **absorbed** in this process…

196.

(narrator speaking of Stelio and Perdita) They were **silent** for a time, **absorbed** in their own **inner tumult** that whirled round within, **penetrating** the very roots of their being…

197.

(narrator speaking) the **power** in the life of the man who wanted to lay claim to the entire universe so as not to die…

198.

(narrator speaking) trying to cheer the **poet** by appealing to his **rebellious spirit**…

199.

(narrator speaking of Stelio) His whole being was concentrated in the **effort** of representing the extraordinary **feeling** that possessed him with the greatest possible **intensity**. Since he was only able to speak about himself and about his own world, he wanted at the very least to find an **ideal image** that would encapsulate the most perfect qualities of his **art** and would demonstrate visually to his disciples that unconquerable force and **desire** that impelled him through life.

200.

(narrator speaking of Stelio) it is essential to **assert** one's Self and to magnify one's **dreams** of **beauty** and of **power**.

201.

(Daniele Glauro speaking to Stelio) "do you see how the **mysterious** process of **artistic** creation are working upon you, and how those thoughts of yours which are about to emerge into the light are being led by some infallible **instinct** that will enable you to choose the most perfect means of **expression**, a sign of the most lofty style from the midst of so many different forms? Because you are having to **work** out your own **ideas**…"

202.

(Daniele Glauro speaking to Stelio) The shadow of the **mysterious** accompanied that **sensual** act. That was how you signified the character of all of your **work**. No **sensuality** is more **ardent** than yours, but your senses are so sharp that even while they delight in appearances, they **penetrate** the very depths until they touch the heart of mystery… You have **insights** beyond the veil on which life has painted the voluptuous **images** that you enjoy so much. You bring together within yourself that which appears to be irreconcilable, you join two opposite poles without any apparent effort, consequently today you provide an example of a life that is complete and all-powerful.

203.

(Stelio speaking) …the gift of **love** and creativity that which my eyes drank in, my **inner sight transformed** into a **deep**, lasting impression.

204.

(narrator speaking of Stelio) And his **willpower** created a new spark…

205.

(Stelio speaking) …charged with **renewed power** and able to take both his life and his **work** into his **inspired** hands.

206.

(Stelio speaking) … there is a **spontaneous**, constant **desire** for **ideal harmony**, as there is within the **soul** of a **pure artist**.

207.

(Stelio speaking) A kind of rhythmic **intelligence** within the **imagination** takes over the process of image-making and shapes those **images** in accordance with some **secret idea**, pushing them towards some premeditated **goal**. This **intelligence** possesses hands that work wonders in shaping light and dark into a never-ending **work** of **beauty**, and her **dreaming** is incorporated into her work, while from that same dream, where all of the inheritance of the past is transfigured, she draws the web of inimitable allegory that enfolds her. And since in the entire universe only **poetry** is **truth**, he who knows how to see poetry and bring her to him with the **strength** of his mind is close to understanding the **secret** of victory in life.

208.

(narrator speaking) …desperate to break the bond of their daily servitude and **discover** the **wild freedom** of **joy** or **pain**.

209.

(narrator speaking of Stelio) At that moment he saw his **ideal image** complete and alive within himself, and he depicted it in the language of **poetry**…

210.

(narrator speaking) that **image** of **nature** served to make the **dream** of **art** even more precious…

211.

(narrator speaking) **inner light** that **inspired** thoughts or **dreams**…

212.

(narrator speaking) people were able to see the world with **new** eyes, to **feel**, think and **dream** with new **souls**. It was the greatest gift of **Beauty** made manifest. It was the victory of **Art** the **Liberator** over the poverty and anxiety and tedium of every day. It was a happy interval during which **pain** and need ceased to exist, when the clenched fist of **Destiny** seemed to be slowly prised open.

213.

(narrator speaking of Stelio) stirred by the breath of the crowd, his **soul** felt able to create gigantic works of **art**. And the still unformed **work** he was **nourishing** within himself gave a **proud** shudder of life, as his eyes caught sight of the great actress standing against the globe of the constellations, the **muse** with the voice that knew how to reveal…

214.

(Stelio speaking) my mind stayed in a state of **solitary ecstasy**…

215.

(Stelio speaking) the **image** of **art** as the first **artists** saw it in their **sincere**, **childish** eyes

---

216.

(Stelio speaking) the **artist** shows us the first signs of **longing** in a **spirit** that has suddenly **discovered** the **boundless** possibilities of life.

217.

(Stelio speaking) What are the notes that those **beautiful, sensitive** hands reveal…

218.

(narrator speaking) the woman who would incarnate in her **changeable** being his future **imaginings** of **beauty** , the woman who would bear the word of **enlightenment**…

219.

(Stelio speaking) She convinces us each day to perform the act that generates our species: the **effort** of going further, unceasingly. She shows us the possibility of **pain transformed** into the most effective form of **inspirational energy**…

220.

(Stelio speaking) The creators are the **mysterious** channels through which **Nature** fulfills her **eternal longing** for things that she cannot herself form from her moulds. And so, continuing the Divine Mother's **work**, their minds are **transformed** into a likeness of the **divine** mind, as Leonardo says. And since creative force flows constantly into their fingertips like sap to the jeweled fruit of trees, they create with **joy**.

221.

(narrator speaking of Stelio) He understood what it meant for him to be **alone** with the white, **silent images** in that indescribably lyrical moment.

222.

(narrator speaking of Stelio) He thought he could **feel**... the presence of **destiny** that was about to give his being a new **impulse**, perhaps to arouse it to a marvelous act of **will**.

223.

(Foscarina replying to Stelio) **genius** of that great **artist** who had seemed as **inspired** and tireless as any of the old masters...

224.

(narrator speaking of Stelio) He saw her as quite **singular** and self-contained, **free** from the petty constraints of habit, living her own separate life, like a great **work** upon which style had imprinted its indelible seal. He saw her set apart, like one of those figures that stand out against a clear, **deep** background, distanced from ordinary life, locked in her own **secret** thoughts. Before the **intensity** of that **inner life** he felt a kind of **passionate impatience** not unlike that of the man filled with **curiosity** who finds himself faced with something that tempts him...

225.

(narrator speaking of Stelio's thoughts) He had **expressed** his **ideas** of **beauty** through his craftsmanship…

226.

(narrator speaking of Stelio) All his **strength**, all his **pride** and all his **desires**…

227.

(Stelio thinking to himself about Perdita) With your fantastic imagination, you have always led my **desire** along the rainbow of your smile towards a special kind of glowing **youthfulness** that you have chosen and kept for me alone.

228.

(Foscarina speaking) All I ask is to serve that **ideal**…

229.

(Foscarina speaking) He carried out his **work** in the teeth of the storm. He **suffered**, **loved** and **struggled alone** with his **faith**, his **passions** and his **genius**…

230.

(narrator speaking about Foscarina) as though she were seeing that brave, **painful** life whose liver had **nourished** the creatures of his **art** with his own warm blood.

231.

(narrator speaking of Stelio) Once again the **expressive power** of her prophetic lips aroused an **ideal image** from some indefinable depths that rose up as though from a tomb before the **poet's** gaze, and took on the color and breath of life.

232.

(narrator speaking of Stelio and Foscarina) They burned together in everlasting **truth**, they heard the melody of the world pass through their luminous **ecstasy**.

233.

(narrator speaking of Stelio and Foscarina) They thought they had lived beyond all human limits, and that in that instant there was an **unknown** vastness before them that they could **absorb** like drinking an **ocean** in a single gulp.

234.

(narrator speaking of Stelio) He was **silent**, lost in that world of **ideal**, intent on calculating the **effort** needed to bring it into being.

235.

(narrator speaking of Stelio) In the communication that had taken place between his **soul** and that of the crowd, something **mysterious**, almost holy, had happened. Something greater and stronger had been added to the **feelings** that he had about his habitual self. An **unknown power** had seemed to converge within him, destroying the boundaries of his **individual** personality and giving his lone **voice** the quality of a chorus. There really was **beauty** in the masses, and only a **poet** or a **hero** could draw out flashes of it. When that beauty was revealed by a sudden clamour in the theatre or in a public place or in a trench, then a torrent of **joy** would swell the heart of the man who had known how to provoke it with his **poetry**, or his speech or by brandishing his sword. So the words of a poet communicating with a crowd of people could be as **powerful** an action as a hero's deeds. It was an action that could create immediate **beauty** in the darkness of the manifold **soul**, just as a gifted **sculptor** can take a lump of clay and with just a touch of his **talented** hands turn it into a **divine** statue. Then, the long **silence**, spread over the finished poem like a sacred veil, would cease. The substance of life would no longer be created by immaterial symbols, life would be depicted in its entirety by the poet, the world would become flesh, rhythm would quicken into a throbbing, breathing form, **ideas** would be uttered in all of their fullness of **strength** and **freedom**.

236.

(Stelio speaking) Everybody who **feels** some kind of obscure need to rise up through **Art**, out of the dungeon of their daily lives where they are confined and **suffer.**

237.

(narrator speaking) Like a **hero**, the **composer** had carried out an act of **liberation.**

238.

(Stelio speaking) To follow the **impulse** of my heart, to obey my own **instincts**, to listen to the **voice** of **nature** within me: that is my one, supreme law!

239.

(Stelio speaking) **expressing** the sound, **young will** that had triumphed over all **obstacles**

240.

(narrator speaking about Foscarina) her cry of **sensuality** and **freedom** rose up to strike the heart of the sun.

241.

(narrator speaking in reference to Stelio) In the **work** of **art** of the future, the source of **inspiration** will never run dry. Art was as endless as **beauty** in the world. There were no limits to **strength** or **desiring**. **Search**, find, go further, keep going further.

242.

(narrator speaking in reference to Stelio) An extraordinarily **beautiful**, **pure** form emerged from that **effort**, **alive** and shining with unbearable happiness… Oh to be able to **express** it, to show it to mankind…

243.

(narrator speaking about Stelio) **instinct** in him rushed to the fore, agitating and dragging with it all the **images** in his mind in the impetus with indescribable **tumult**.

244.

(narrator speaking about Stelio) A thought that came as **spontaneously** as **instinct** swept him...

245.

(narrator speaking about Foscarina) during all that she had **struggled** for so **intensely** and that happened during her **wanderings**...

246.

(Foscarina reflecting to herself) Oh, if only one day I could fashion wings for you for your highest flight of all, out of that **strength** of mine which has been tempered by storms, out of all the strong, clear things that **pain** and **rebellion** have revealed in the depths of my **soul**, from the very best of me!

247.

(narrator speaking about Stelio) all his **senses** sought to **transcend** human limitations, sought the **joy** that is beyond all **obstacles**; they became sublime, able to **penetrate** the furthest **mysteries** of all, to **discover** the very darkest **secrets**, to derive pleasure from pleasure as one **harmony** follows another, they were instruments of miracle, **infinitely powerful**, as real as **death** itself.

248.

(narrator speaking about Stelio) Silently he lay without moving as revulsion flooded through his whole being… He thought that the **silence** was waiting for a scream.

249.

(Foscarina speaking to Stelio) I am **troubled** by a heart that is **alive** and, oh Stelio, so alive and hungry and **tormented** that you cannot imagine…

250.

(narrator speaking about Foscarina) seized hold of her own **courage**.

251.

(narrator speaking of Stelio and Foscarina) They were both face to face with the **truth**, with their naked, throbbing hearts.

252.

(Foscarina speaking to Stelio) to have **silently, fervently** gone on with the continual **effort** of giving some **beauty**, some **harmony** to my spirit… to have shivered as I spoke **immortal** words out there on stage so many times… to have toiled ceaselessly, to have tried always to reach a simpler, more **intense** form of **art**… and to have defended against everybody and everything this **idealism** hidden in my **soul**…

253.

(Stelio speaking to Foscarina) I was happy, my heart was completely open, I was **dreaming** and **hoping**, I felt **reborn**…

254.

(Foscarina speaking to Stelio) Yes, you were happy to breathe again and be **free**, to **feel** your own **youth** out there in the wind and the daylight.

255.

(narrator speaking about Stelio) With words and with **music**, the **Poet** was reshaping the **ideal** unity of life.

256.

(narrator speaking about Stelio) devoured by the **urge** to fulfill his own **destiny** to the utmost.

257.

(narrator speaking about Richard Wagner) fixed on his own star and **determined** to force the world to recognize it.

258.

(Stelio speaking to Daniele Glauro) A **new** melody, something amazingly **powerful** that came to him very faintly in his earliest **youth** and which he could never master, that would suddenly split open his heart like a mighty sword.

259.

(Daniele Glauro speaking) He has the **divine power** of **fervor** and he has the taste for all-powerful **strength** and the **passion**…

260.

(Daniele Glauro speaking) He was drawn to Richard Wagner by great **natural energy**.

261.

(narrator speaking of Stelio) spread the **power** of his **oceanic soul** across the world… **transformed** into **infinite** song the **essences** of the Universe for the religion of men.

262.

(Stelio speaking of Richard Wagner) Do you know that it was in Venice that Richard Wagner had his first conversation with **death**, twenty years ago, when he was composing *Tristan*? Consumed by a desperate **passion**, he came to Venice to die from it in **silence**, and he **wrote** that amazing second act, here which is really a hymn to **eternal** night. Now his **destiny** has brought him back to these lagoons.

263.

(narrator speaking of Stelio) Stelio was moving almost **instinctively**…

264.

(narrator speaking of Stelio) Stelio paused, **listening** with such **intense concentration** that his friend was astounded and felt as though he were watching him being **transformed** into the very **natural** phenomenon he was observing, and slowly being obliterated by a greater, more **powerful will** that was **absorbing** him and making him like itself.

265.

(Stelio speaking) If I could only take it in its living state from the **eternal** spring, from the **mystery** of **Nature** itself, from the very **soul** of universal things!

266.

(Stelio speaking) so that a **new** form of **art** can appear.

267.

(Stelio speaking) I don't want to revive an ancient form, I want to **invent** a **new** one, something that will come from my own **instincts** and the **genius**… just as the Greeks did when they created the marvelously **beautiful** edifice that can never be imitated, which is their theatre.

268.

(Stelio speaking of Richard Wagner) and so will be open to a greater **vision** of an even greater **joy**.

269.

(Stelio speaking to Daniele Glauro) Oh Daniele, how can I give you some **idea** of the **work** that is alive inside me…? How can I communicate the life and the **infinitely** fluid **mystery** that are within me?

270.

(narrator speaking) It towered over **solitude**…

271.

(narrator speaking about Stelio) The whole line of the melody had come to him, it was his now, **immortalized** in his **spirit** and in the world. Of all things living, nothing seemed more alive to him than that. His very life yielded to the **boundless energy** of that **idea** in sound, the generating force of that seed which would be **infinitely developed**.

272.

(Stelio speaking) the rightness of his own **intuition**. 'Imagine,' he said, 'the interval between two symphonic movements where all the motifs endeavor to **express** the **inner essence** of the characters whose **struggle** is depicted in the drama, to reveal the intimate source of the action, like for example Beethoven's grand overture in *Leonora* or in *Coriolanus*. The **musical silence** throbbing with rhythm is the living, **mysterious** atmosphere that is the only place where words of **pure poetry** can appear.

273.

(Stelio speaking) the **truth** of the hidden being that is working within them.

274.

(Stelio speaking) I am creating an **ideal** atmosphere around **heroic** myths in which the whole of **Nature's** life is vibrating so that in every one of their actions all the **power** of their preordained **destiny** seems to converge…

275.

(Stelio speaking) I want **Nature** all around them to be seen as their ancient forefathers saw her, as the **passionate** actress in an **eternal** drama.

276.

(Stelio speaking) Have you ever thought about the mighty Schliemann at the moment when he uncovered the most dazzling treasure that **Death** had ever hidden in the obscurities of earth for centuries, for millennia? Have you ever thought that someone else might be able to see that terrifying, super-human spectacle, some **young**, **fervent** spirit, some **poet**, some creator, you, me perhaps?

277.

(narrator speaking of Stelio) He was all on fire, trembling, **feeling** himself suddenly carried away by the storm of his **imagination**. His **visionary** eyes reflected the gleam… Creative **energy** flowed through his spirit like blood through his heart. He was an actor in his own drama, his tone and his movements signified **transcendental passion** and **beauty**, going beyond the **power** of the spoken word, the limitations of the letter. His brother hung on his lips, trembling before the sudden splendor that was bringing his **divining** thoughts into being.

278.

(Stelio speaking) And so that **ideal** life which you have **nourished** yourself takes on the shape and outline of reality!

279.

(Stelio speaking to Daniele Glauro) The **new soul** will burst open the circle of iron that binds it, with a **strength** of purpose generated by madness, a lucid madness that is like **ecstasy**, like the most profound of **Nature's visions**.

280.

(narrator speaking about Stelio) He was astonished by the… **unexpected discovery** that was coming to light…

281.

(Foscarina speaking) such an **urge** to **rebel**…

282.

(narrator speaking of Foscarina) as **alive** as the very hand that had penned them, beating like her **impatient** pulse.

283.

(narrator speaking of Foscarina's thoughts) Lorenzo Arvale used to create his statues in the fullness of **strength** and **inspiration**, **oblivious** to the lightning bolt that was about to strike him down.

284.

(narrator speaking of Foscarina's thoughts) her thoughts and that **pure voice** and the **mystery** of **art** combined to make **divine** life appear in that great studio...

285.

(narrator speaking of Foscarina) She is sure of herself, she is mistress of her own **strength**.

286.

(narrator speaking of Foscarina) She is made to… arouse their **curiosity** and **inspire** their **dreams**.

287.

(narrator speaking of Foscarina) Her **bold**, cautious **instinct** is already leading her…

288.

(narrator speaking of Stelio) He breathed in her **soul**, as though it were elemental, and received such ineffable fullness of life in return that it

Blake Bazel, M.S.

was as though a melodious river of **mysterious** things were rising out of her and out of the depths of the day and pouring into his **overflowing** heart.

289.

(narrator speaking of Foscarina) She knew how completely he abandoned himself to every wave of **feeling**…

290.

(narrator speaking of Foscarina) But she also knew the marvelous speed and diversity of **feeling** and **thinking** that made his mind so impossible to grasp. There was always something voluble, fluctuating and **powerful** in him that suggested the double, yet diverse **images** of fire and water.

291.

(narrator speaking of Foscarina) There was always a **boundless desire**…

292.

(narrator speaking of Stelio) She was for him a source of **inspiration** for **visions** and **images**, like hills and woods and rain. He drank **mystery** and **beauty** from her as he did from everything else in the universe. And already he had moved on, he was in **search** of something **new**, his open, seeing eyes were looking round at the miracle to **wonder** at and to adore.

293.

(narrator speaking of Foscarina) to tell her about his **feelings** and his **dreams** before she could reach out her aching heart to that landscape.

294.

(narrator speaking of Foscarina) One instant of **intensity** had happened, and she was waiting for the next.

295.

(narrator speaking of Stelio) the magnificent illusions that he had given to his own **soul** so as to **inspire** it to go beyond its own limits and beyond its own **destiny**…

296.

(Foscarina speaking to Stelio) Such strange **silence**. Like **ecstasy**!

297.

(narrator speaking of Stelio) And as he breathed and his heart beat among the branches, all his **senses** were filled with the **pleasure** of it, the communion between his life and the life of the trees **deepened**... the spell of his **imagination** renewed the task of the first maker of wings...

298.

(narrator speaking of Stelio) he had lit up fleeting moments with **passion** and **beauty** and had contagiously communicated the **strength** of his own vitality to those around him, raising their **spirits** to a superior sphere...

299.

(narrator speaking) It was indeed **beautiful**, and like all **natural** things it was **mysterious**...

300.

(narrator speaking of Foscarina) a new concordance of her **inner forces,** from a **mysterious** direction of her **reawakened will.**

301.

(narrator speaking) some great thing was taking place in **silence**.

302.

(Foscarina speaking to Stelio) it was the obscure presence of the **strength** that was to develop in me later, that **difference** and special quality that **Nature** had bestowed on me…

303.

(Foscarina speaking to Stelio) I had the most extraordinary **visions** that **dreams** have ever **awakened** in my **soul**. I saw things I can never forget: I saw **images** from my own thoughts and **instincts** superimpose themselves on the real forms of things that were around me. There, before my staring eyes… I saw the world of my own **expressiveness** begin to take shape… The first lines of my **art** were developed in that state of agitation, exhaustion, feverishness and revulsion, when my **senses** had become what I might describe as malleable… There was a natural **desire** in me to shape that material, to breathe life into it, to fill the hollow of a mould…

304.

(narrator speaking of Stelio) He, the man of **joy**, felt drawn to so much accumulated **pain**, to so much **pride** and humility, such **struggle** and such conquests.

305.

(Foscarina speaking) In the evening, on stage, as I performed I would remember one or other of them and I used to have such **powerful feelings** about how far away and lonely they were out in the peaceful countryside under the stars, that I could hardly speak.

306.

(Foscarina speaking) From that time onwards, in the most **impassioned** moments of my **work** on stage, **images** from remembered landscapes have always come to me, especially when I succeeded in communicating a great shudder to the spectators through the **pure power** of **silence**...

307.

(Foscarina speaking) The words flowed with **strange** ease, almost **spontaneously**...

308.

(Narrator speaking of Foscarina) the **strength** of her **passion** and her **desire**, reinforced by an idea of justice, appeared to be about to accomplish a miracle.

309.

(Stelio speaking to Foscarina) I have a **work** to finish **writing** and a life to live according to **Nature's** plan… I talked to you at length about my life and about the **impulse** that drives it towards its **destiny**.

310.

(narrator speaking of Foscarina) Her alert **sensitivity** watched and **listened** at the inaccessible doorway to his thoughts. At certain times she reached the point of being able to **feel** another life throbbing beneath his heartbeat.

311.

(narrator speaking of Foscarina) Her **soul**, intent on creating a **new feeling**…

312.

(Stelio speaking to Foscarina) 'Michelangelo,' he said, '**concentrated** all the **efforts** of human thought into a tiny dent in the marble. And just as a river fills up a hollowed palm, so the **eternal mystery** that surrounds us all filled up that little space which the Titanic **sculptor** chiseled into the marble taken from the mountains, and it has stayed there and become more **powerful** through the centuries.'

313.

(narrator speaking of Foscarina) She reached out to the **Creator**, eager for **poetry** and **knowledge**. For him, she was the **ideal** figure of a **listening**, understanding woman.

314.

(narrator speaking of Stelio) illuminated by an inner flame, as though some supreme **hope** had **unexpectedly** appeared in him or some **immortal truth** been revealed to him.

315.

(narrator describing Foscarina's feelings and thoughts of Stelio) feeling his **sensuous** body so profoundly gripped by the genesis of an **idea**. She stayed **silent**, waiting. She worshipped the **unknown** thoughts in the head that was resting on her knees. But she understood his great **struggle** better one day, after she had been **reading**, when he told her about the Exile.

316.

(Stelio speaking to Foscarina) **Imagine** Dante Alighieri, already filled with his **visions** on the road into exile, a **restless** pilgrim… always watchful, his eager eyes always open, **troubled** by the **inner struggle** that would result in his gigantic **work**.

317.

(Stelio speaking to Foscarina) Through his **senses**, multifaceted life in its many forms poured into his mind and transfigured the abstract **ideas** crowded in there into living **images**. Everywhere he went, **unexpected** sources of **poetry** flowed from beneath his aching feet. The **voices**, forms and **essence** of the elements entered that **secret** toil and increased it with countless sounds, colours, movements and **mysteries**. Fire, Air, Water and Earth all contributed to the **divine poem**.

318.

(narrator speaking of Foscarina) Then she began to feel that her own life depended on that all-**absorbing work**, as though drop by drop her **soul** were entering into the character in his drama, and her features, her stance, her gestures, the tone of her voice were combining to create the figure of the **heroine** 'living beyond life'.

319.

(narrator speaking of Foscarina) **Art** fostered the appearance of the **new feeling** for which she had prepared.

320.

(Foscarina's thoughts on Stelio) He will read the **silent** words in my **soul** that he will put in the mouth of his creation...

321.

(narrator speaking of Foscarina) she sometimes emerged with a **wild desire** to break the spell, to become **different**, to detach herself from the **image** that was supposed to resemble her, to break the lines of **beauty** that held her in...

322.

(narrator speaking of Stelio) Then he **loved** her for the **unexpected visions** that she aroused in him, for the **mysterious sense** of inner happenings that she communicated to him...

323.

(narrator speaking of Stelio) The scene kept appearing and vanishing again, as though a torrent of **poetry** were rushing over it.

324.

(narrator speaking of Foscarina) The blindness of **immortal** statues was in her eyes. She saw herself **sculpted** in the vast **silence**, and she felt the quivering of the silent crowd, as their heartstrings were gripped by the sublime **power** of her appearance.

325.

(Stelio speaking to Foscarina) You must call Cassandra out of her sleep, you must feel her ashes coming alive in your hands, you must see her in your **vision**.

326.

(Stelio speaking to Foscarina) Your living **soul** must touch her ancient soul and blend with it and make one single soul…

327.

(Stelio speaking) In the world of **ideal** origins, there is no more **powerful** thing, no reproductive organ of greater virtuosity. And there is no greater **delight** for an active brain than watching how such **energy** develops…

328.

(narrator speaking of Stelio) There was a profound analogy between the **spontaneous** formation of myths and his **instinctive** need to animate everything that came into contact with his **senses**.

329.

(narrator speaking of Stelio) But his **soul** could find no rest, and nothing could free it from its burden.

330.

(narrator speaking of Foscarina) She realized again that **desire**, unconquerable desire, was the forger of all her illusions and all those **hopes** that seemed to help her to accomplish 'that which **love** cannot do…'

331.

(Foscarina's thoughts of Stellio) seeing him possessed by his **ideals** and **concentrating** intently all his **energies** on the **effor**t taking place in his mind.

332.

(narrator speaking) the wide-ranging **imaginings** of the **poet**…

333.

(Foscarina's thoughts) she began to **feel** the same anxiety, confusing reality with **fantasy** in her mind.

334.

(Stelio's thoughts) He should be **experimenting** every hour, every moment, fighting, growing **stronger**, **asserting** himself against the forces that destroy, diminish, spoil and contaminate. Every hour, every minute he should keep his eye trained on the target, and **focus** all of his **energies** on that **goal**, ceaselessly, **relentlessly**.

335.

(Stelio speaking) those marvelous **images** were passing through my mind accompanied by waves of **music**…

336.

(Stelio speaking) To **express** myself! That was what I had to do! Even the most lofty **visions** are worthless if they cannot be demonstrated and condensed into living forms. I have everything to create. I am not pouring my **essence** into inherited moulds. My **work** is completely **new**. I can't and won't obey anything except my own **instinct** and the **genius**…

337.

(Stelio speaking) But that **spontaneous** gesture served as an **expression** of my gratitude to the Man who made my **spirit** feel the necessity of being **heroic** in its **struggle** for **freedom** and creativity.

338.

(narrator speaking) A **spirit** of life was flowing through the loneliness, powerful **hopes** were disturbing the **silence**. It was as though some natural **desire** to rise upwards were passing like an **awakening**...

339.

(narrator speaking of Stelio) the young man was seized by a feverish **impatience** to act, by his haste to go on **writing**, by his need to complete his task. His capacity to **work** seemed to be increasing.

340.

(narrator speaking) The **images** of life evoked by the **Poet**, and the ancient names of **immortal energies** circulating in the Universe, and the **desire** of mankind to **transcend** the circle of their daily **torment** to seek comfort in the splendour of **Idealism**, and the **wishes** and **hopes** and **daring** and **effort** in that place...

341.

(narrator speaking) only that song of **freedom** and victory could touch the heart of the man who wanted to create with **joy** . 'Forward! Higher, even higher!'

342.

(narrator speaking of Foscarina) She threw her head back, with one of those **spontaneous** gestures of hers that seemed to be breaking some bond or **freeing** her of some burden.

343.

(Foscarina speaking to Stelio) Now that the shape of your **work** is complete, what you need is peace for your writing… Haven't you always been able to **write** at home? You will never be able to quiet the anxiety that chokes you anywhere else.

344.

(Stelio speaking to Foscarina) what really matters is for the **work** to develop in austere **silence**, what counts is slow, indomitable tenaciousness, hard, **pure solitude** and the absolute **devotion** of flesh and **spirit** to the **Ideal** that we want to bring to life amongst men forever as a conquering force.

345.

(narrator speaking about Foscarina's thoughts of Stelio) the firm **resolve** to go beyond himself and force his **destiny** onwards **relentlessly**.

346.

(narrator speaking of Stelio) Seated, not to rest but to contemplate another task, he was gazing at Life with his **powerful** eyes, shining with the light of a **free** soul. **Silence** rose up to him from all the forms around him…

347.

(Stelio speaking) the man who keeps his own fire blazing to **strengthen** his own force.

348.

(Stelio speaking) One thing **alone** is constant: my **courage**. I never sit down, except to rise again.

CHAPTER 17
SENTIMENTAL EDUCATION
by Gustave Flaubert

349.

(narrator speaking of Frédéric) a **deeper yearning**, an aching **curiosity** which knew no bounds.

350.

(narrator speaking of Frédéric) he drifted into **infinite** , **dream joy**.

351.

(narrator speaking of Charles) He conceived a **passionate interest** in metaphysics and made rapid progress in the subject, for he approached it with **youthful energy** and the **pride** of an **intelligence** tasting **freedom** for the first time. He **read**... everything the library had to offer. He even stole the key, to obtain the books he wanted.

352.

(narrator speaking of Frédéric) After **discovering** some medieval plays, he embarked on the **reading** of memoirs...

353.

(narrator speaking of Frédéric and Charles) They went on to the bridge where they could talk more **freely**.

354.

(narrator speaking of Frédéric) The first of his **dreams** had come to nothing.

355.

(narrator speaking of Frédéric) Frédéric had not done any **writing** recently; his literary opinions had **changed**; he now prized **passion** above all else…

356.

(narrator speaking of Frédéric) Sometimes he felt only that **music** was capable of **expressing** his **secret troubles**, and then he **dreamt** of symphonies…

357.

(Frédéric speaking) **Love** is the stuff of **genius**. Great **emotions** produce great **works** of **art**.

358.

(narrator speaking of Frédéric) This **idea tormented** Frédéric ...

359.

(narrator speaking of Frédéric) Frédéric and his companion **boldly** asked to see the man...

360.

(narrator speaking of Pellerin) Pellerin used to **read** every available book on aesthetics, in the **hope** of **discovering** the true theory of **Beauty**, for he was convinced that once he had found it he would be able to paint masterpieces. He surrounded himself with every conceivable accessory... going out into the street to seek **inspiration**, thrilling with **joy** when he had found it... to **dream** of another which would be even finer. Tortured by a **longing**... His robust **pride** prevented him from **feeling** any discouragement...

361.

(narrator speaking of Frédéric) to be **unique** of their kind and charged with **meaning**, like a sacred script.

362.

(narrator speaking of Frédéric) His aim was the **emancipation** of the **arts**, the sublime…

363.

(narrator speaking of Frédéric) **Solitude** opened up once again, beneath the new immensity of his **desire**.

364.

(narrator speaking of Frédéric) Then he was seized by one of those tremblings of the **soul** in which you feel yourself transported into a higher world. An extraordinary **talent**, object unknown, had been bestowed upon him. He asked himself in all seriousness whether he was to be a great **painter** or a great **poet**…

365.

(narrator speaking of Frédéric) Frédéric spent hours at a time **alone** in the studio. The quiet of this spacious room—where there was nothing to be heard but the scampering of the mice—the light falling from the ceiling, and even the rumbling of the stove, filled him at first with a **sense** of **intellectual** well-being.

366.

(narrator speaking of Frédéric and Deslauriers) They argued about the **immortality** of the **soul**...

367.

(narrator speaking of Dussardier) He said it in a way that **silenced** them for a moment; some were taken aback by this **innocent** declaration, some perhaps recognized the unspoken **desire** of their hearts.

368.

(narrator speaking of Frédéric) Frédéric, standing by the stove, gazed at the walls, the whatnot, the floor; and **delightful visions** flitted through his memory, or rather before his eyes.

369.

(narrator speaking of Madame Arnoux) ...**absorbed** in her own thoughts.

370.

(narrator speaking of Madame Arnoux) But surely, she argued, one must derive a **deeper pleasure** from moving people directly, in person; from seeing the **emotions** of one's own **soul** entering into theirs.

371.

(narrator speaking of Frédéric) Then he felt her gaze **penetrating** his **soul**, like those great rays of sunlight which go down into the very depths of the water.

372.

(narrator speaking of Frédéric) In the meantime an **inner breath** seemed to carry him beyond himself; it was a **longing**… a **yearning** for **self-dedication**…

373.

(narrator speaking of Frédéric) But there was only one place in the world where he could turn them to account: Paris! Because, so he believed, **art**, **learning**, and **love**—those three faces of **God**, as Pellerin would have said—were available exclusively in the capital.

374.

(narrator speaking of Frédéric) In a sudden explosion of **youthful feeling**...

375.

(the artist speaking) Because everything exists in **nature**, and so everything is a legitimate subject for **painting**. It's just a matter of striking the right note—and I've **discovered** the **secret**.

376.

(narrator speaking of Frédéric) He bought the works of his favorite **poets**... because he had countless **plans** for **work**.

377.

(narrator speaking of Frédéric) Frédéric felt glad to be **alive**; he could scarcely restrain himself from singing; he felt an **urge** to **express** himself, to perform...

378.

(narrator speaking of Madame Arnoux) she made simple, **penetrating** remarks which showed a charming **intelligence**. She liked traveling, the sound of the wind in the woods...

379.

(Pellerin speaking) **Imagine** that these things are splendid treasures, sumptuous gifts. The head a little to the right. Perfect! Don't move! That majestic attitude suits your type of **beauty**.

380.

Pellerin speaking) Nonsense! The **artist's** red isn't the same as the red of the common man!

381.

(narrator speaking of Pellerin) He started sketching in the main outlines, and he was so preoccupied with the great **artists** of the Renaissance that he began talking about them. For a whole hour he **dreamt** aloud of those wonderful lives, full of **genius**...

382.

(narrator speaking of Frédéric) Frédéric, filled with inexplicable **self-confidence**...

383.

(narrator speaking of Frédéric) his enthusiasm for the scenery and masterpieces of Italian **art**...

384.

(narrator speaking of the Citizen) the Citizen thought Arnoux full of **feeling** and **imagination**...

385.

(narrator speaking) **searching** for **artistic improvements**...

386.

(Frédéric speaking to Madame Arnoux) How can you possibly imagine that somebody with my habits and my **intellectual** needs could bury himself in the country to play cards, supervise builders, and walk about in clogs? Whatever for... Do you think that when I've always **longed** for the ultimate in **beauty**, tenderness, and charm, and when I've finally found this **ideal**, when the **vision** prevents me from seeing any other...

387.

(narrator speaking of Frédéric) He told her about … how a woman's face used to shine in his **poetic paradise**…

388.

(narrator speaking of Monsieur Dambreuse) Then, with the detachment of a superior mind, he talked about the exhibition at which he had seen Pellerin's picture. He considered it an **original** work, which had come off very well.

389.

(narrator speaking of Frédéric) Frédéric brooded over this **idea**, like a dramatist **writing** a play.

390.

(narrator speaking of Frédéric and Rosanette) They thought that they were far from other people, completely **alone**.

391.

(narrator speaking of Frédéric and Rosanette) Standing side by side on some hillock, and breathing in the wind, they felt their **souls** filling with a sort of **pride** in a **freer** life, a surge of **strength**, an inexplicable **joy.**

392.

(narrator speaking of Frédéric and Rosanette) The solemnity of the forest took hold of them; and there were hours of **silence** when, abandoning themselves to the gentle rocking of the springs, they lay sunk in a calm intoxication.

393.

(narrator speaking of Frédéric and Rosanette) They found **pleasure** in everything, pointing out to each other gossamer threads hanging from bushes, holes full of water in the middle of stones, a squirrel on a branch, a couple of butterflies flying after each other, or else, twenty yards away, under the trees, a doe walking placidly along, with a noble, gentle air, her fawn at her side. Rosanette felt like running after it to give it a kiss.

CHAPTER 18
KALLOCAIN
by Karin Boye

394.

(narrator speaking) there is a something that feels this to be insufficient and that has **inspired** and **envisioned** another labor within me... [I] have been **deeply** and almost **painfully** involved. That labor will be completed when I have finished my book. Consequently, I realize how unreasonable and **irrational** my scribblings must seem in comparison to all rational and practical thinking; yet **write** I must.

395.

(narrator speaking) Perhaps I would not have **dared** earlier.

396.

(narrator speaking) I can feel freer than in **freedom**.

397.

(narrator speaking) The opportunity to **write** has been given me...

398.

(narrator speaking) certain moments returned as riddles and forced me to **wonder**, solve, and solve again.

399.

(narrator speaking of Rissen) At times he might appear feverishly excited, his words bubbling over each other... or at other times lapse into long unmotivated pauses, withdrawn in thought...

400.

(narrator speaking) A scientist too, in his laboratory, can be **courageous**...

401.

(narrator speaking) We've been granted something **different**, and more than ordinary mortals...

402.

(narrator speaking) experienced the moment of **exaltation**...

403.

(narrator speaking of Karrek) He was made up only of **will power**…

404.

(narrator speaking) My **longing** for **adventure**…

405.

(narrator speaking) I had an almost **wild longing**…

406.

(narrator speaking) …my **curiosity**.

407.

(Linda speaking to Leo) creation takes place in us… otherwise everything is without **meaning**.

408.

(Linda speaking to Leo) She had her own melody… She was not like anyone else.

409.

(narrator speaking) On my way to the examination hall, **wild fantasies** had flashed through my mind…

410.

(narrator speaking) The night was breathing, the night was **alive**, and as far out in **infinity** as I could see, the stars pulsated like hearts and filled the empty space with wave after wave of vibrating life.

411.

(narrator speaking) I was convinced that anything could happen.

412.

(narrator speaking) I was participating in the creation of a **new** world.

413.

(narrator speaking) Although I was walking all by myself here above ground, here below the stars, I had a **peculiar sensation** I was not alone. As I was on my way to the **unknown** to **seek** the world's living **meaning**...

414.

(narrator speaking) one has **felt** that one's pulses are being driven by a heart in the cosmos...

415.

(Rissen speaking) I know that what I am goes somewhere.

CHAPTER 19
THE VIRGIN AND THE GIPSY
by D.H. Lawrence

416.

(narrator speaking) Then lo and behold! The vicar, who was somewhat distinguished as an essayist and a **controversialist**...

417.

(narrator speaking of Lucille and Yvette) They seemed so dashing and **unconventional**...

418.

(narrator speaking of Lucille and Yvette) The two girls were both **determined**...

419.

(narrator speaking of Yvette) So, with **curiosity**, she followed the woman up the steps of the caravan...

420.

(narrator speaking of Yvette) … in her own kind of **strength**, her own kind of understanding.

421.

(narrator speaking of Yvette) A flame of **passion**…

422.

(narrator speaking of Yvette) Yvette began to realize the other sanctity of herself, the sanctity of her **sensitive**…

423.

(narrator speaking of Yvette's thoughts) a hard, **defiant pride** of its own…

424.

(narrator speaking of Yvette) It was some hidden part of herself which she denied: that part which **mysteriously**…

425.

(narrator speaking of Yvette) Yvette too had a **free-born** quality.

426.

(narrator speaking of Yvette's thoughts) While it endured, she was spellbound to it, in revulsion.

427.

(narrator speaking of the gipsy) he was too much master to himself…

428.

(narrator speaking of Yvette) She liked the **mysterious** endurance in him, which **endures** in opposition, without any idea of victory. And she liked that **peculiar** added **relentlessness**…

429.

(narrator speaking of Yvette) she **loved** with **curious tenderness**…

430.

(narrator speaking of Yvette) It was part of her nature to get these fits of **yearning**…

431.

(narrator speaking of the gipsy) And like a thing **obsessed**…

CHAPTER 20
THE AWAKENING
by Kate Chopin

432.

(narrator speaking of Mrs. Pontellier) Mrs. Pontellier's eyes were quick and bright; they were a yellowish brown, about the color of her hair. She had a way of turning them swiftly upon an object and holding them there as if lost in some inward maze of **contemplation** or thought.

433.

(narrator speaking of Mrs. Pontellier) Mrs. Pontellier had brought her sketching materials, which she sometimes dabbled with in an unprofessional way. She liked the dabbling. She felt in it satisfaction…

434.

(narrator speaking of Mrs. Pontellier) She handled her brushes with a certain ease and **freedom** which came, not from long and close acquaintance with them, but from a **natural** aptitude.

435.

(narrator speaking of Mrs. Pontellier) … **contradictory impulses** which impelled her. A certain light was beginning to dawn dimly within her…

436.

(narrator speaking of Mrs. Pontellier) It moved her to **dreams**, to thoughtfulness…

437.

(narrator speaking of Mrs. Pontellier) In short, Mrs. Pontellier was beginning to realize her position in the universe as a human being, and to recognize her relations as an **individual** to the **world within** and about her.

438.

(narrator speaking) But the beginning of things, of a world especially, is necessarily vague, tangled, **chaotic**, and exceedingly disturbing. How few of us ever emerge from such beginning! How many **souls** perish in **tumult**!

The **voice** of the **sea** is seductive; never ceasing, whispering, clamoring, murmuring, inviting the **soul** to **wander** for a spell in abysses of **solitude**; to lose itself in mazes of inward **contemplation**.

The voice of the sea speaks to the soul. The touch of the sea is **sensuous**, enfolding the body in its soft, close embrace.

439.

(narrator speaking of Mrs. Pontellier) Even as a child she had lived her own small life all within herself. At a very early period she had apprehended **instinctively** the dual life—the outward existence which conforms, the **inward life** which **questions**.

440.

(narrator speaking of Mrs. Pontellier) That summer at Grand Isle she began to loosen a little the mantle of reserve that had always enveloped her. There may have been—there must have been **influences**, both subtle and apparent, working in their several ways to induce her to do this…

441.

(narrator speaking of Mrs. Pontellier) Edna had a **sensuous** susceptibility to **beauty**.

442.

(narrator speaking) made frequent and **unexpected** inroads.

443.

(narrator speaking of Mrs. Pontellier) the **absorbed expression** which seemed to have seized and fixed every feature…

444.

(narrator speaking of Mrs. Pontellier) It was when the face and figure of a great tragedian began to haunt her **imagination** and stir her **senses**. The **persistence** of the infatuation lent it an aspect of **genuineness**… colored it with the lofty tones of a great **passion**.

445.

(Madame Ratignolle speaking) She is not one of us; she is not like us.

446.

(narrator speaking of Mrs. Pontellier) One piece which that lady played Edna had entitled "**Solitude**." It was a short, plaintive, minor strain. The name of the piece was something else, but she called it "Solitude." When she heard it there came before her **imagination** the figure of a man standing beside a desolate rock on the **seashore**.

447.

(narrator speaking of Mrs. Pontellier) Edna was what she herself called very fond of **music**. Musical strains, well rendered, had a way of evoking pictures in her mind.

448.

(narrator speaking of Mrs. Pontellier) But the very **passions** themselves were aroused within her **soul**, swaying it, lashing it, as the **waves** daily beat upon her splendid body.

449.

(narrator speaking of Mrs. Pontellier) But that night she was like the little tottering, stumbling, clutching **child**, who all of a sudden realizes its **powers**, and walks for the first time **alone**, **boldly** and with overconfidence. She could have shouted for **joy**.

450.

(narrator speaking of Mrs. Pontellier) A feeling of **exultation** overtook her, as if some **power** of significant import had been given her to control the working of her body and her **soul**. She grew **daring**…

451.

(narrator speaking of Mrs. Pontellier) She turned her face **seaward** to gather in an impression of space and **solitude**, which the vast expanse of water, meeting and melting with the moonlit sky, conveyed to her excited fancy. As she swam she seemed to be reaching out for the unlimited in which to lose herself.

452.

(narrator speaking of Mrs. Pontellier) A thousand **emotions** have swept through me tonight. I don't comprehend half of them. Don't mind what I am saying; I am just **thinking** aloud.

453.

(Robert speaking) a spirit that has haunted these shores for ages rises up from the Gulf. With its own **penetrating vision** the **spirit** seeks some one mortal worthy to hold him company, worthy of being **exalted** for a few hours into realms of the semicelestials. His **search** has always hitherto been fruitless, and he has sunk back disheartened, into the **sea**. But tonight he found Mrs. Pontellier.

454.

(narrator speaking of Mrs. Pontellier) … reviving again with an **intensity** which filled her with an incomprehensible **longing**.

455.

(narrator speaking of Mrs. Pontellier) She was happy to be alive and breathing, when her whole being seemed to be one with the sunlight, the color, the odors, the luxuriant warmth of some perfect Southern day. She liked then to **wander** alone into **strange** and **unfamiliar** places. She **discovered** many a sunny, sleepy corner, fashioned to **dream** in. And she found it good to dream and to be **alone**.

456.

(narrator speaking of Mrs. Pontellier) Then Edna sat in the library after dinner and **read** Emerson until she grew sleepy. She realized that she had neglected her reading, and **determined** to start **anew** upon a course of **improving** studies…

457.

(narrator speaking of Mrs. Pontellier) she drew satisfaction from the **work** in itself.

458.

(narrator speaking of Mrs. Pontellier) when she **listened**, was led on… fresh promises which her **youth** held out to her.

459.

(narrator speaking of Mrs. Pontellier) I know I shall like it, like the **feeling** of **freedom** and **independence**.

460.

(narrator speaking of Mrs. Pontellier) There was the shock of the **unexpected** and the unaccustomed.

461.

(narrator speaking of Mrs. Pontellier) She felt as if a mist had been lifted from her eyes, enabling her to look upon and comprehend the significance of life…

462.

(narrator speaking of Mrs. Pontellier) There came over her the acute **longing** which always summoned into her **spiritual vision** the presence of the beloved one, overpowering her at once with a **sense** of the unattainable.

463.

(narrator speaking of Victor) He seemed to have abandoned himself to a reverie, and to be seeing pleasing **visions**…

464.

(narrator speaking of Mrs. Pontellier) … her **strength** and expansion as an **individual**…

465.

(narrator speaking of Mrs. Pontellier) She lived with them a whole week long… and gathering and filling herself with their **young** existence.

466.

(narrator speaking of Mrs. Pontellier) I have got into a habit of **expressing** myself.

467.

(narrator speaking of Mrs. Pontellier) She felt like some **new-born** creature, opening its eyes in a familiar world that it had never known.

468.

(narrator speaking) The **artist** must possess the **courageous soul** that **dares** and **defies**.

CHAPTER 21
SELECTED WRITINGS
Gerard de Nerval

Angélique

469.

(narrator speaking) Voyage in **search** of a **unique** book.

470.

(narrator speaking) **wander** through its principal streets...

471.

(narrator speaking) all bejeweled, festooned and inlaid with gold, it was like some bouquet of flowers plucked from some unimaginable **paradise**.

472.

(narrator speaking) I was **confident** that I would be able to **paint** his portrait and **write**...

Creativity Defined

473.

(narrator speaking) I have **read** books…

474.

(narrator speaking) I **wrote** two series of articles…

475.

(narrator speaking) This **eccentric** and ever-so-slippery figure cannot hope to elude my **painstaking** investigation for very long.

(narrator speaking) The last of this **courageous** band…

476.

(narrator speaking) **imagination** and **energy** are written all over his face…

477.

(narrator speaking) … I made an extremely **interesting discovery**…

478.

(narrator speaking) I therefore took advantage of the occasion to mix **pleasure** with research.

479.

(narrator speaking) ... all flow together into a region where you can still **imagine**...

480.

(narrator speaking) ... the most **beautiful** pastoral **adventures** in the world...

481.

(narrator speaking) ... composed entirely in her hand, which is perhaps even more **daring** than Rousseau's own *Confessions*.

482.

(narrator speaking) From the age of thirteen onwards, Angélique de Longueval, whose temperament was at once **dreamy**...

483.

(Angélique speaking) The following morning, I made so **bold** as to try…

484.

(narrator speaking) … the poet Théophile de Viau often used to repair to **dream**.

485.

(narrator speaking) … my **journey** in **search** of the castle of his ancestors, an excursion I am undertaking so as to be able to provide a precise description of the setting of his **adventures**…

486.

(narrator speaking) But are not the incarnations of **ideal beauty** as **eternal** as **genius**?

Blake Bazel, M.S.

Sylvie

487.

(narrator speaking) I felt myself **alive**…

488.

(narrator speaking) … we at last breathed the **pure** air of **solitude**… drunk with **poetry** and **love**—

489.

(narrator speaking) She had to appear a queen or **goddess**: above all, she had to lie beyond reach.

490.

(narrator speaking) Amid our **renewed fantasies** of Alexandria, we would occasionally brandish the torch of the **gods** of the underworld, momentarily illuminating the darkness with a trail of sparks.

491.

(narrator speaking) … **boundless** vitality of the various brilliant wits who gathered there. Wits such as these—**lively, unpredictable**, occasionally sublime—are an inevitable feature of periods of **renewal**…

492.

(narrator speaking) My **ideal** was henceforth within reach…

493.

(narrator speaking) the innocent festivals of my **youth**…

494.

(narrator speaking) We thought we were in a **paradise**.

495.

(narrator speaking) She resembled Dante's Beatrice, smiling upon the **poet** as he **wandered** at the outer reaches of her blessed abode.

Blake Bazel, M.S.

496.

(narrator speaking) … the thirst for **knowledge** will live on for ever, the spur of all vitality and all action!

497.

(narrator speaking) Aurélie was pouring all her charm and **inspiration** into some verses feebly inspired by Schiller…

Aurélia

498.

(narrator speaking) **Dream** is a second life.

499.

(narrator speaking) I shall attempt to transcribe the impressions of a lengthy illness that took place entirely within the **mysteries** of my own mind— although I do not know why I use the term illness here, for so far as I am concerned, I never felt more fit. At times I believed my **strength** and **energy** had redoubled; I seemed to know everything, understand everything; my **imagination** afforded me **infinite delights**. Having recovered what men call reason, must I lament the loss of such joys?

500.

(narrator speaking) I have taken the **inventions** of **poets** too seriously and have made a Laura or a Beatrice out of an ordinary woman of our century...

501.

(narrator speaking) Apuleius' *Golden* Ass and Dante's *Divine Comedy* are the **poetic** models of such studies of the human **soul**.

502.

(narrator speaking) imprinted it with the seal of **eternity**.

503.

(narrator speaking) That night I had a **dream** which confirmed this **idea**. I was **wandering** through an immense building made up of several rooms, some being used as study halls, others devoted to conversation or philosophic debate. Out of **curiosity**…

504.

(narrator speaking) it seemed to me that I understood everything, that the **mysteries** of the world were being revealed to me in these final hours.

505.

(narrator speaking) I began to scan the sky for a certain star I thought I knew, as if it had some influence over my fate. Having located it, I continued on my way, following the streets where I could see it ahead of me, forging onwards as it were, towards my **destiny** and wanting to keep the star in view until the moment **death** was to strike… My friend seemed to be exerting superhuman **strength** to get me to move on; he was growing ever larger in my eyes and taking on the features of an apostle.

506.

(narrator speaking) The **idea** has often occurred to me…

507.

(narrator speaking) As I walked along, I chanted a **mysterious** hymn…

508.

(narrator speaking) a **writer's mission**…

509.

(narrator speaking) and if I had not set myself a **goal** I believe useful, I would stop here, rather than attempt to describe what I subsequently experienced in a series of **visions**…

510.

(narrator speaking) This heavenly **vision**, by a phenomenon everyone has experienced in certain **dreams**…

511.

(narrator speaking) the **images** of every land appeared distinctly and simultaneously, as if my **powers** of attention had been multiplied without losing their sense of detail…

512.

(narrator speaking) their vigorous, **resolute** air and the **energetic** cast of their features reminded me of those **independent** warrior races who live in the mountains or on islands rarely visited by strangers; and yet they had managed to maintain their fierce **individuality**…

513.

(narrator speaking) The various vistas, interlaced by long trains of climbing vegetation, were as enchanting to the eye and as pleasing to the mind as the sight of a luscious oasis. Amid this unsuspected **solitude**…

514.

(narrator speaking) **penetrating** into the **mysteries** of these sanctuaries.

515.

(narrator speaking) they **inspired** a kind of love in me that **transcended** preference or **desire**, a **love** that epitomized all the vague exhilaration of **youthful passion**.

516.

(narrator speaking) I melted into tears, as if remembering a lost **paradise**.

517.

(narrator speaking) Such was the **vision**…

518.

(narrator speaking) A subsequent **dream** confirmed my views.

519.

(narrator speaking) … like those **ideal** types fashioned by **painters** after several different models so as to capture the complete range of **beauty**.

520.

(narrator speaking) This **dream**, which started out so happily, caused me no end of perplexity.

521.

(narrator speaking) I went even further; I tried to shape the body of my beloved out of clay; every morning I had to start my **work** all over again, for the lunatics, jealous of my **joy**, took delight in smashing the **image**.

522.

(narrator speaking) … the first germs of creation were **struggling** into existence.

523.

(narrator speaking) All of a sudden a wondrous **harmony** echoed through our **solitudes**… in this **divine** chorus.

524.

(narrator speaking) as they went through their **transformations**...

525.

(narrator speaking) ... carrying with it the **hopes** for a **new** creation.

526.

(narrator speaking) But upon **reflection**...

527.

(narrator speaking) The **idea** came to me to **search** my **dreams** for an answer, but *her* **image**...

528.

(narrator speaking) I gathered up all my **willpower** in order to **penetrate deeper** into the **mystery** whose veils I had begun to lift.

529.

(narrator speaking) I had disturbed the **harmony** of that magical universe from which my soul drew the certainty of **immortal** life. Perhaps I was accursed for having attempted to **penetrate** into a terrible **mystery** in violation of **divine** law…

530.

(narrator speaking) a sublime **dream** in the shadowy reaches of **infinity**…

531.

(narrator speaking) Then I saw sculpted **images** from antiquity, first in sketchy outline, then gradually taking on firmer contours, and finally resolving themselves into symbols of sorts whose **meaning** I struggled to grasp.

532.

(narrator speaking) These **visions** and the ensuing **reflections** which occupied my hours of **solitude** produced in me a **feeling**…

533.

(narrator speaking) during this sort of self-examination in which I was engaged, the most distant events came back to my mind with a particular sharpness.

534.

(narrator speaking) … opened my mind to a more precise appreciation of certain **truths** which I had not firmly enough gathered into my **soul**. For those who have no **faith** in **immortality** with all its **joys** and **sorrows**…

535.

(narrator speaking) The succession of **visions** which had come to me during sleep…

536.

(narrator speaking) I was again filled with **hope**.

537.

(narrator speaking) A splendid **vision** came to me as I slept.

Blake Bazel, M.S.

538.

(narrator speaking) I ascribed a **mysterious** significance…

539.

(narrator speaking) I initially **imagined**…

540.

(narrator speaking) This **idea** led to another…

541.

(narrator speaking) One night I was talking and singing in a kind of **ecstasy**.

542.

(narrator speaking) That night I had a marvelous **dream**…

543.

(narrator speaking) My **dream** ended with the fond **hope** that peace would at last be granted us.

544.

(narrator speaking) In this way I gradually gathered the **courage** to undertake a **bold** venture. I decided to fix upon my **dreams** and **discover** their **secret**. I said to myself, armed with sufficient **willpower**, why should I not at last be able to force open these mystic gates and master my **sensations** instead of submitting to them?

545.

(narrator speaking) After several minutes of drowsiness, a **new** life begins, **freed** from the bounds of time and space...

546.

(narrator speaking) I made **efforts** to seize the **meaning** of my **dreams**... Such were the **inspirations** of my nights...

547.

(narrator speaking) I am happy with the convictions I have acquired...

CHAPTER 22
INFERNO
August Strindberg

548.

(narrator speaking) WITH A SAVAGE **JOY** I walked away from the Gare du Nord...

549.

(narrator speaking) ... **divined** my hidden thoughts, followed the development of my **plans** and kept a... eye on my **struggles** to explore **unknown** realms....

550.

(narrator speaking) A **free** man once again, I felt a sudden release of the **soul's energy** and was sent **soaring** above...

551.

(narrator speaking) ... a victory that constituted the fulfillment of a **youthful dream** cherished by all my literary contemporaries and compatriots but realized by myself alone...

552.

(narrator speaking) But now, the theatre **inspired** in me…

553.

(narrator speaking) … I had decided to attain the summit of **knowledge**…

554.

(narrator speaking) … and won the only **immortality** allowed to a mortal man.

555.

(narrator speaking) … a constant reminder of the price I had paid for my triumph.

556.

(narrator speaking) … **liberation** from those sordid bonds…

557.

(narrator speaking) A zone of **silence** and **solitude** was set up around me. It was the calm of the desert, awesome and horrible, in which, out of bravado, I deliberately provoked the **unknown** to combat, to wrestle with it body against body, **soul** against soul.

558.

(narrator speaking)… **young artists** who felt no necessity for restraint in that atmosphere.

559.

(narrator speaking) … it was necessary for me to break down the **obstacles** in my **path** before winning the victor's crown.

560.

(narrator speaking) I bowed before the storm, **resolving** to pull myself upright again at the first opportunity.

561.

(narrator speaking) … I engaged in a correspondence that provided further sustenance for my continuing **search**.

562.

(narrator speaking) … **wandering** in a country far from home.

563.

(narrator speaking) … only one man possessed **genius**, an untamed **spirit** who had won a respected name for himself.

564.

(narrator speaking) If the **pride** that had made me…

565.

(narrator speaking) … the **desire** to purify my **individual being** and to cultivate my personality in **solitary meditation**…

566.

(narrator speaking) I was happy to find a shelter for the long winter evenings, even though the scabrous tone of the conversation there caused me to **suffer deeply**.

567.

(narrator speaking) The **unknown** became a personal acquaintance.

568.

(narrator speaking) … and the **knowledge** that I was being supported by **unknown powers** supplied me with a fund of **energy** and **self-confidence** that pushed me on to **efforts** I had never thought myself capable of til then.

569.

(narrator speaking) I was now **reborn** in another world where no one could follow me… my **dreams** at night assumed the form of omens.

570.

(narrator speaking) … with the result that my **work** came to a halt and a period of **idleness** ensued.

571.

(narrator speaking) Judge of my **ecstasy**… when faced with this **revelation** amounting almost to a miracle.

572.

(narrator speaking) I **discovered** a tombstone of classic simplicity and **beauty**.

573.

(narrator speaking) Encouraged by my successful **experiments**...

574.

(narrator speaking) ... **independence, freedom** to continue my studies...

575.

(narrator speaking) Don't all **discoveries** have their price?

576.

(narrator speaking) the only way that leads to Wisdom.

577.

(narrator speaking) I was able to buy books and things to help me in my studies in natural history, among other things a microscope which revealed to me the **mysteries** of life.

578.

(narrator speaking) … a state of **soul** rather than a view based on theories; a disordered **chaos** of **sensations** more or less condensed into **ideas**.

579.

(narrator speaking) … the **feelings** that were rising within me.

580.

(narrator speaking) … granting myself the same **freedom** that I felt I must allow to others.

581.

(narrator speaking) Proudly aware of my clairvoyant **powers**, I there **penetrated** to the very heart of the **secret** of creation…

582.

(narrator speaking) I, **alone** and **suffering**…

583.

(narrator speaking) Once introduced into this **new** world where no one could follow me…

584.

(narrator speaking) I therefore informed my friends that I was going to settle at Meudon in order to **write** a book that demanded **solitude** and **silence**.

585.

(narrator speaking) The first consequence of this was an unprecedented expansion of my inner **senses**; a psychic **energy** that insisted on making itself felt. I thought of myself as the repository of limitless **powers**, and **pride** insinuated into my head…

586.

(narrator speaking) I was sure of having said something **new**, great, and **beautiful**.

587.

(narrator speaking) ... a **fantasy** play I had **written**.

588.

(narrator speaking) ... assuming some form of **invention** by **unknown powers**...

589.

(narrator speaking) This state of **uncertainty**...

590.

(narrator speaking of another artist) With his **lively** mind, cosmopolitan outlook, and **bold** manner...

591.

(narrator speaking of another artist) ... his **self-confidence** and assured manner...

592.

(narrator speaking of another artist) ... a **youthful** escapade...

593.

(narrator speaking of another artist) I **discovered** he had a rare **intelligence**... coupled with an unbridled **sensuality**.

(narrator speaking of Francis Schlatter) ... leading, without knowing it, an **independent** existence.

594.

(narrator speaking) I **discovered** that my **mysterious** friend...

595.

(narrator speaking of another artist) During the time my comrade had been able to **re-educate** himself completely and had found the time to **change** his method of **painting**...

596.

(narrator speaking of another artist) His **patience** and **endurance** were positively **heroic**.

597.

(narrator speaking) We both heard an **inner voice** telling us that our **destinies** were to fulfill themselves separately…

598.

(narrator speaking) Indeed, it proved absolutely **new** to me, and now that my mind was prepared for it I was able to **absorb** the contents of this extraordinary book.

599.

(narrator speaking) … I was seized with **ecstatic** admiration as I **listened** to the **voice** of this angelic giant of a previous century being interpreted to me by the most profound of all French **geniuses**.

600.

(narrator speaking) I was prepared for a higher existence.

601.

(narrator speaking) The **pride**, first aroused by my intimacy with the **powers**, continued to grow unceasingly…

602.

(narrator speaking of another artist) **Artist** that he was, he responded to the **beauty** of the lines, one after another… The longer we stood gazing, the more real, **alive**, and awesome became the apparition.

603.

(narrator speaking) … it was all far too **natural**—but there was etched in my **soul** the impression of something abnormal…

604.

(narrator speaking about another artist) I was immediately struck by the **beautiful** lines of a charcoal drawing hanging on one wall.

605.

(narrator speaking) Here was a **new art** revealed, an art taken from **nature** herself!

606.

(narrator speaking) … inaugurating a **new** form of **art**, rich with **youth** and **hope**

607.

(narrator speaking) … may the **harmony** of matter and **spirit** be **born** again.

608.

(narrator speaking) Nothing is ever done in this world without the consent of the **powers**.

609.

(narrator speaking) Sometimes at night I had **dreams**… revealing **secret**s to me.

610.

(narrator speaking) … the **joyous** laughter of the **young** girls playing down below, invisible beneath the trees, touched my heart and called me back to life.

611.

(narrator speaking) I decided to **struggle**, to defend myself…

612.

(narrator speaking) I had just turned off into the Luxembourg Gardens, which were in full flower and as **beautiful** as a fairy tale…

613.

(narrator speaking) I live by **improvising** as I go along; life is more **fun** that way!

614.

(narrator speaking) I looked upon him more as an **ideal** figure than a real person.

615.

(narrator speaking) the cultivation of one's self must therefore be viewed without question as the supreme and final aim of our existence.

616.

(narrator speaking) To **struggle** for the preservation of my Self… a duty dictated by the conscience bestowed on me by the grace of my **divine** protectors.

617.

(narrator speaking) I **concentrated** all my **will**…

618.

(narrator speaking) … that great **artist** who extends his own being as he creates, making sketches and rejecting them, **reworking** abortive ideas… Often he has taken great steps forward by **inventing**…

619.

(narrator speaking) … these thoughts were turning over in my mind…

620.

(narrator speaking) My host was an **artist**; his house was **beautiful**; moreover it was a home in the true sense, full of connubial **love**, ravishing **children**… liberal **ideas**, an atmosphere of **beauty**…

621.

(narrator speaking) A **poetical** metaphor that perhaps contained the whole **truth**.

622.

(narrator speaking) I could **sense** the approach of some imminent **change** in my **destiny**.

623.

(narrator speaking about his daughter) … gazed into the depths of my **soul**…

624.

(narrator speaking) I was rooted to the spot as I crossed the threshold, overcome by the **vision**.

625.

(narrator speaking) The whole room was furnished in a way that made it a **poem**, the **inspiration** of a **soul** only partly of this earth.

626.

(narrator speaking) I was able to force the **sensations** aroused in me by Swedenborg's book back into the **deepest** recesses of my **soul**.

627.

(narrator speaking) I retraced my steps, plunged in thoughts about this combination of random details that, when taken together, made up one great unity, **awe-inspiring**...

628.

(narrator speaking) My **reading** of Swedenborg occupied me during the daytime...

629.

(narrator speaking) I recognized my own observations, my own **sensations**, my own **ideas** to such an extent that his **visions** appeared to me to be part of reality... it was enough to **read** what was set down and then compare that with one's own experiences.

630.

(narrator speaking) In order to remain **independent**...

631.

(narrator speaking) Ever since my youth I have always devoted my morning **walk** to preparing the day's work ahead. I never allowed anyone to accompany me, not even my wife.

632.

(narrator speaking) Indeed, in the morning my **spirit** is filled with a delicious **harmony**, a sort of expansive mood verging on **ecstasy**. I don't walk, I fly… It is my hour of **meditation**…

633.

(narrator speaking) I was preoccupied with my thoughts…

634.

(narrator speaking) … it was the **will** of the powers that we should take that **path**. It was a period of **experiment**…

635.

(narrator speaking) … set me **free**.

636.

(narrator speaking) … I had been in a state of revolt…

637.

(narrator speaking) … to live in… **freedom**

638.

(narrator speaking) … to yield to the **impulse** of the moment

---

639.

(narrator speaking) … every conception or **idea** of a thing is formed by **reflecting** on the **differences** between **contraries** regarded in different ways and from different points of view.

640.

(narrator speaking) Are they **visions, intuitions, inspirations?**

641.

(narrator speaking) … a **freethinker**…

642.

(narrator speaking) Have you noticed in moments of **solitude**, during the night, or even in broad daylight, how your memories rise from the past, trembling as though newly resurrected, one by one and two by two?

643.

(narrator speaking) ...for the **enlightenment** I **desired**.

CHAPTER 23
TESS OF THE D'URBERVILLES
Thomas Hardy

644.

(narrator speaking) **Ideal** and real clashed slightly as the sun lit up their figures against the green hedges and creeper-laced house-fronts; for, though the whole troop wore white garments, no two whites were alike among them.

645.

(narrator speaking) … each had a **private** little sun for her **soul** to bask in; some **dream**, some affection, some hobby, at least some remote and distant **hope** which, though perhaps starving to nothing, still lived on, as hopes will.

646.

(narrator speaking) Tess Durbeyfield at this time of her life was a mere vessel of **emotions**…

647.

(narrator speaking of Tess Durbeyfield) She was… so **expressive**…

648.

(narrator speaking of Tess Durbeyfield's mother) There was a **dreaminess**, a preoccupation, an **exaltation**, in the maternal look which the girl could not understand.

649.

(narrator speaking of Tess Durbeyfield's mother) … regarding him only in his **ideal** presentation…

650.

(narrator speaking of Tess Durbeyfield) … was **silently wondering**…

651.

(narrator speaking of Tess Durbeyfield) … Tess's **pride**…

652.

(Tess speaking to Alec d'Uberville) "Never!" said Tess **independently**...

653.

(Alec d'Uberville speaking to Tess) Very well, Miss **Independence**...

654.

(narrator speaking of Tess and Alec) They followed the road with a **sensation** that they were **soaring** along in a supportive medium, possessed of **original** and **profound thoughts**, themselves and surrounding **nature** forming an organism of which all of the parts **harmoniously** and **joyously interpenetrated** each other. They were as sublime as the moon and stars above them, and the moon and stars were as **ardent** as they.

655.

(narrator speaking of Tess Durbeyfield) ... beginning to **feel** in the moonlight **journey**.

656.

(narrator speaking) … **persistently beautified** it; til the erratic motions seemed an inherent part of the irradiation and the fumes of their breathing a component of the night's mist; and the spirit of the scene, and of the moonlight, and of **Nature** seemed **harmoniously** to mingle with the **spirit** of wine.

657.

(narrator speaking of Tess Durbeyfield) … as became visitors to a person who had made a **transcendent** conquest…

658.

(narrator speaking of Tess Durbeyfield) She thought, without exactly wording the thought, how **strange** and **god-like** was a **composer's power** who from the grave could lead through sequences of **emotion**, which he alone had felt at first, a girl like her who had never heard of his name and never would have a clue to his personality.

659.

(narrator speaking of Tess Durbeyfield) The only exercise that Tess took at this time was after dark; and it was then, when out in the woods, that she seemed least **solitary**. She knew how to hit to a hair's-breadth that moment of evening when the light and the darkness are so evenly balanced that the constraint of day and the suspense of night neutralize each other, leaving absolute mental **liberty**. It is then that the plight of being alive becomes attenuated to its least-possible dimension.

660.

(narrator speaking of Tess Durbeyfield) It was they that were out of **harmony** with the actual world, not she. Walking among the sleeping birds in the hedges, watching the skipping rabbits on a moonlit warren, or standing under a pheasant-laden bough… She had been made to break an accepted social law, but no law known to the environment in which she fancied herself such an anomaly.

661.

(narrator speaking) … by reason of the charm which is acquired by woman when she becomes part and parcel of outdoor **nature** and is not merely an object set down therein as at ordinary times.

662.

(narrator speaking of Tess Durbeyfield) Tess, with a **curiously** stealthy yet **courageous** movement…

663.

(narrator speaking of Tess Durbeyfield) She was not an existence, an experience, a **passion**, a structure of **sensations**, to anybody but herself.

664.

(narrator speaking of Tess Durbeyfield) If she could have been but just created, to **discover** herself...

665.

(narrator speaking of Tess Durbeyfield) ... her **soul's desire** was to continue that offence...

666.

(narrator speaking) ... **Nature**, who respects not the social law...

667.

(narrator speaking of Tess Durbeyfield) ... she did not mind speaking **freely**.

668.

(narrator speaking of Tess Durbeyfield) The eye of maternal affection did not see them in its **vision** of higher things.

669.

(narrator speaking of Tess Durbeyfield) Symbols of **reflectiveness** passed into her face…

670.

(narrator speaking of Tess Durbeyfield) Yet even now Tess felt the pulse of **hopeful** life still warm within her…

671.

(narrator speaking of Tess Durbeyfield) … some spirit rose within her automatically as the sap in the twigs. It was unexpended **youth**, surging up **anew** after its temporary check and bringing with it **hope** and the **invincible instinct** towards **self-delight**.

672.

(narrator speaking of Tess Durbeyfield) … through which it was necessary to pass on her **journey**, now in a direction almost opposite to that of her first **adventuring**.

673.

(narrator speaking of Tess Durbeyfield) … the **sense** of being amid **new** scenes…

674.

(narrator speaking of Tess Durbeyfield) Her face had latterly changed with **changing** states of mind, continually fluctuating between **beauty** and ordinariness, according as thoughts were gay or grave.

675.

(narrator speaking of Tess Durbeyfield) She declared that she could stand it, and her zest and willingness…

676.

(narrator speaking of Angel) … that was a vocation which would probably afford an **independence** without the sacrifice of what he valued even more than a competency—**intellectual liberty**.

677.

(narrator speaking of Angel) But he soon preferred to **read** human **nature**…

678.

(narrator speaking of Angel) For the first time of late years he could **read** as his musing inclined him…

679.

(narrator speaking of Angel) He grew away from old associations and saw something **new** in life and humanity. Secondarily, he made close acquaintance with phenomena which he had before known but darkly—the seasons in their moods, morning and evening, night and noon, winds in their different tempers, trees, waters and mists, shades and **silences**, and the **voices** of inanimate things.

680.

(narrator speaking of Tess Durbeyfield) The **exaltation** of which she had described as being producible at **will** by gazing at a star came now without any determination of hers; she undulated upon the thin notes of the second-hand harp, and their **harmonies** passed like breezes through her, bringing tears into her eyes. The floating pollen seemed to be his notes made visible, and the dampness of the garden the weeping of the garden's **sensibility**.

681.

(narrator speaking of Angel's thoughts of Tess) She was **expressing** in her own native phrases—assisted a little by her Sixth Standard training—**feelings** which might almost have been called... the ache of modernism. The perception arrested him less when he **reflected**...

682.

(narrator speaking of Tess Durbeyfield's thoughts of Angel) ... a decidedly **bookish, musical, thinking young** man...

683.

(dairyman speaking of Angel Clare to Tess) "Mr. Clare," said the dairyman emphatically, "is one of the most **rebellest** rozums you ever knowed...

684.

(narrator speaking of Tess Durbeyfield) ... suggested to her that it was largely owing to her supposed **untraditional newness**...

685.

(narrator speaking of Angel's thoughts of Tess) regard of an exceedingly **novel**, fresh, and interesting…

686.

(narrator speaking of Tess and Angel) The spectral, half-compounded, aqueous light which pervaded the open mead impressed them with a **feeling** of isolation**,** as if they were Adam and Eve.

687.

(narrator speaking) There was a **reflective silence.**

688.

(narrator speaking of Tess Durbeyfield) … she who knew herself to be more **impassioned** in **nature**, cleverer, more **beautiful** than they…

689.

(narrator speaking of Angel) … **resolve** upon a **plan** for plunging into that world **anew.**

690.

(narrator speaking of Tess Durbeyfield) Upon her **sensations** the whole world depended to Tess; through her existence all her fellow-creatures existed, to her.

691.

(narrator speaking of Angel) It was on the **impulse** of the moment that he **resolved**…

692.

(Angel speaking of Tess) She's brim full of **poetry**—actualized poetry, if I may use the expression. She *lives* what paper-poets only write…

693.

(narrator speaking of Angel's thoughts of Tess) It was for herself that he loved Tess—her **soul**, her heart, her substance…

694.

(narrator speaking of Angel's thoughts of Tess) Her unsophisticated open-air existence required no varnish or conventionality to make it palatable to him. He held that education has as yet but little affected the beats of **emotion** and **impulse**…

695.

(narrator speaking of Tess and Angel) a fitful white streak of steam at intervals upon the dark-green background denoted intermittent moments of contact between their secluded world and modern life.

696.

(narrator speaking of Tess Durbeyfield) … formed a season through which she lived in **spiritual** altitudes more nearly approaching **ecstasy** than any other period of her life.

697.

(narrator speaking) …as if she saw something **immortal** before her.

698.

(narrator speaking of Tess Durbeyfield) Some of the dairy-people, who were also out-of-doors on the first Sunday evening after their engagement, heard her **impulsive** speeches, **ecstasized** to fragments…

699.

(narrator speaking of Tess Durbeyfield) With the **impulse** of a **soul** who could **feel** for kindred **sufferers**…

700.

(narrator speaking of Tess Durbeyfield) She was ashamed of herself for her gloom of the night, based on nothing more tangible than a sense of condemnation under an arbitrary law of society which had no foundation in **nature**.

701.

(narrator speaking of Tess Durbeyfield) Tess went onward with **fortitude**…

702.

(narrator speaking of Tess Durbeyfield) … but it was time to **rest** from **searching**, and she **resolved** to stay, particularly as it began to rain.

703.

(narrator speaking of Angel) … and the **vision** sent the *aura* through his veins…

CHAPTER 24
GERTRUDE
Hermann Hesse

704.

(narrator speaking) ... to taste the good and the bad to the full and to make for oneself a more **individual**, unaccidental and inward **destiny** alongside one's external fate...

705.

(narrator speaking) ... my **inner life** has been of my own making.

706.

(narrator speaking) I was given the **freedom** to **discover** my own inclinations and **talents,** to fashion my inmost **pleasures** and **sorrows** myself and to regard the future not as an alien higher power but as the **hope** and product of my own **strength.**

707.

(narrator speaking) I was **destined** to be most strongly affected and dominated by... **music.** From that moment on I had a **world of my**

own, a sanctuary and a heaven that no one could take away from me...

708.

(narrator speaking) ... it takes possession of all of your **strength** and **emotions**, and during the time it lives in you... it brings the world into **harmony** with you...

709.

(narrator speaking) That is where my dearest and brightest **dreams** have ranged—to hear for the duration of a heartbeat the universe and the totality of life in its **mysterious**, innate **harmony**.

710.

(narrator speaking) Within me I can **sense** the urgent admonition and thirsting **desire** for one **pure**, pleasing, essentially holy sound and its fading away...

711.

(narrator speaking) ... an **inward voice** also told me that it was good and right to make a career of that which filled my thoughts and alone gave me real **pleasure**.

712.

(narrator speaking) … the **uncertain** career of an **artist**…

713.

(narrator speaking) … the **stronger** grew my **will**…

714.

(narrator speaking) … my **desire** became even **stronger**.

715.

(narrator speaking) … I **suffered** and **enjoyed** the **emotions**…

716.

(narrator speaking) … one of the wonderful hours of premature creative **desire** enveloped me like ether… where all my **senses** were sharpened and on the alert.

717.

(narrator speaking) … the **intense concentration** required to give a melody the proper, **singular**, no longer fortuitous movement and **solution**… there would never be anything as **desirable** and important in my life as the return of such hours of clarity and creativeness.

718.

(narrator speaking) At the same time I also had periods of **daydreaming** when I **improvised** on the violin and enjoyed the intoxication of fleeting impressions and **exalted** moods.

719.

(narrator speaking) … to wrestle strenuously and **resolutely** with the **secrets** of form…

720.

(narrator speaking) I also partly realized at that time that true creativity isolates one and demands something that has to be subtracted from the enjoyment of life.

721.

(narrator speaking) … I was **free**.

722.

(narrator speaking) … I had considered myself some kind of a **genius** and had considerably underestimated the toils and **difficulties** encountered along the **path** to an **art**.

723.

(narrator speaking) If the old **ideal** had not been **secretly** alive in me…

724.

(narrator speaking) I still looked **longingly**…

725.

(narrator speaking) … my **youth** demanded stormy **emotions** and **excitement**…

726.

(narrator speaking) We again romped through the snow like carefree **children**…

727.

(narrator speaking) I was very **ardent** and was determined to make the most of this opportunity…

728.

(narrator speaking) I began to hum it and **unexpectedly**, **music**, which had so long been a stranger, came back to me like a suddenly revealed star, and my heart beat to its rhythm, and my whole being blossomed and inhaled **new**, **pure** air… I just felt its presence and it **penetrated** my being gently…

729.

(narrator speaking) I **reflected** awhile and then said that I had not thought about my violin for a long time; but now I suddenly did and it gave me great **pleasure**.

730.

(narrator speaking) I thought I now saw my **goal** clearly…

731.

(narrator speaking) In the depths of my **soul**… there was sweet **music**.

732.

(narrator speaking) … the **intense desire** to make **music**, to create. I again often felt the clear vibrations of a rarefied atmosphere, the concentration of **ideas**…

733.

(narrator speaking) I felt that the sudden flashes of **insight** and the **musical** sketches I made during my best hours no longer defined all the rules and laws, but that through assiduous study a narrow but clearly discernible **path** was leading to **freedom**… I **struggled** vainly against **contradictions** and pitfalls…

734.

(narrator speaking) … I enjoyed the **solitude** like a cool, healing drink.

735.

(narrator speaking) I was **alone** and **free** like a bird in the air…

736.

(narrator speaking) … the calm **solitude** surrounded me like a fortress…

737.

(narrator speaking) After I made the **discovery**…

738.

(narrator speaking) … there were also days when it was stormy and inclement within me.

739.

(narrator speaking) … I seemed to see all the glorious **beauty** of the mountains, and everything that my **senses enjoyed**…

740.

(narrator speaking) … whether I experienced **pleasure** and **enjoyment**, or **grief** and depression, both moods seemed clearer and more comprehensible to me. They **freed** themselves from my **soul** and approached me from the outside in the form of **harmonies**…

741.

(narrator speaking) … the almost glasslike brightness and transparency of **feelings**…

742.

(narrator speaking) … everything signified **strength** and sound and **creative release**. **Music** was arising from the turmoil, iridescence and conflict of my **awakened sensibilities**.

743.

(narrator speaking) … with heightened **feelings** of happiness and **joy**, and with a **new** conception.

744.

(narrator speaking) … my **discovered strength**…

745.

(narrator speaking) … it was still **strange** to me and its territory was **unfamiliar**.

Creativity Defined

746.

(narrator speaking) ... I knew it was my own **music, born** and experienced within me...

747.

(narrator speaking) ... **courage** for my next **path** in life.

748.

(narrator speaking of Muoth) ... full of **curiosity**.

749.

(narrator speaking of Muoth)... he had an **instinctive, powerful** way...

750.

(narrator speaking of Muoth) His dark, **searching** eyes...

751.

(narrator speaking of Muoth) ... I am glad when I find something that seems **individual**...

752.

(narrator speaking of Muoth) ... a **sensitive passionate** man who was **suffering**...

753.

(narrator speaking) ... I was also isolated and not fully understood by other people, even if I was **different** from everyone else and separated from most people by fate and my **talents**...

754.

(narrator speaking) I then played my **music** quite **confidently**...

755.

(narrator speaking of Kranzl) ...so **natural**, indeed, almost naïve.

Creativity Defined

756.

(narrator speaking of Kranzl) … to find this man so **natural** and **sincere**.

757.

(narrator speaking) I frequently took out my sonata… Sometimes I found it quite **beautiful**…

758.

(narrator speaking to Muoth) I want to feel that **pleasure** and **pain** arise from the same source, that they are aspects of the same force and portions of the same piece of **music**, each **beautiful** and each essential.

759.

(Marian speaking to narrator) He is an **emotional** man…

760.

(narrator speaking) … a hunger for **music** remained that only **tormented** me unbearably during the violin lessons…

761.

(narrator speaking) … I relapsed into a wonderful **dreamlike** state in which I built **bold** sound edifices, erected magnificent castles in the air… and created **musical** patterns…

762.

(narrator speaking) … I had **visions** of a great symphony…

763.

(narrator speaking) I threw myself into it and lived in a world of **music**.

764.

(narrator speaking) I was sometimes seized by a sudden, fleeting, almost subconscious **desire** for **solitude**…

765.

(narrator speaking) … quiet hours and **creative work**…

766.

(Muoth speaking to narrator) I won't say much—I am not a professor, but it is **beautiful**!

767.

(narrator speaking about himself) ... who **longed** for **love**...

768.

(narrator speaking) I did not want to be like anyone else... I wanted to remain in my own skin...

769.

(narrator speaking) I began to feel **power** within me as my **work** began to have some effect, and I was on the point of becoming **proud**. I had to find some kind of bridge to reach people...

770.

(narrator speaking) ... the world lay before me in its original **divine** light as it does to **children**, and as it appears to us in our **dreams** of **Paradise**.

771.

(narrator speaking) I see all the **goal**s of life and **art**…

772.

(narrator speaking) … the **harmony** and inward rhythm of my life—and trace it back within me to the legendary years of my **childhood**. And when I wanted to express this **dreamlike beauty**…

773.

(narrator speaking) … experienced my **youthful dream** of the **harmony**…

774.

(narrator speaking of Teiser) Only Teiser, with his **childlike simplicity**…

775.

(narrator speaking of Teiser) I felt a sense of kinship with him and the way he looked forward to his long walking holiday, to **freedom** and carefree unity with the sun, air and earth. In the same way I felt **renewed pleasure** at the thought of all the **paths** in my life which lay before me as if illuminated by a brilliant **new** sun…

776.

(narrator speaking) For me too **love** and **work**, **music** and life, were no longer separable.

777.

(narrator speaking) ... I did not know whether it was my **work** or my **love** which impelled and **exalted** me.

778.

(narrator speaking) I continually depicted the unattainable in **strange fantasies**.

779.

(narrator speaking) I sat **meditating** a great deal...

780.

(narrator speaking) How **strange** and lonely was my **path** and how **uncertain** my destination!

781.

(narrator speaking) … that all this **power** and **emotion** should arise from the **restless dreams** and **imagination**…

782.

(narrator speaking) … I was convinced of the quality and **strength** of my **work**. It was **sincere** and **ardent**…

783.

(narrator speaking) … valleys of **youth** and **passion**.

784.

(narrator speaking) … all my **yearning** and **ardor**…

785.

(narrator speaking) … I **visualize** the whole opera on the stage…

786.

(Teiser speaking to narrator) … Muoth has tremendous **energy**.

787.

(narrator speaking) Right up to the present I have never lost the **feeling** of **contradiction** that lies behind all **knowledge**.

788.

(narrator speaking) … the **feeling** of **liberation**…

789.

(narrator speaking) I had thought of a long period of **solitude** among the mountains or of losing myself in hard **work**…

790.

(narrator speaking) I **discovered** many things.

791.

(narrator speaking) I again plunged **deeply** into the swift creative current with feverish intoxication, until I finally emerged to the **free** heights of **feeling**, where **pain** and bliss are no longer separate from each other and all **passion** and **strength** in the **soul** press upward in one steady flame.

792.

(narrator speaking) On the day that I **wrote** my **new** song…

793.

(narrator speaking) … Gertrude's **sensitiveness**…

794.

(narrator speaking) … the **passion** and **longing** of that period confronted me…

795.

(narrator speaking of Gertrude and Heinrich) … they only drew closer through **passion** and in the intoxication of **exalted** hours.

796.

(narrator speaking) When **music** stirred my being, I understood everything without the aid of words. I was then aware of **pure harmony** in the **essence** of life…

797.

(narrator speaking) I then locked myself in my room, played the **passionate** and **yearning music** of my opera, which I suddenly **loved** and understood again, lay awake at nights full of **longing**, and again **suffered** all the former laughable **torments** of **youth** and unfulfilled **desires**...

798.

(narrator speaking of Heinrich) He let his **imagination** run riot...

799.

(narrator speaking of the singer) He sang with **fervor** and **passion**.

800.

(narrator speaking) I **meditated** for a long time about these things...

801.

(narrator speaking) We can then be **gods** for moments, stretch out a commanding hand and create things which were not there before and which, when they are created, continue to live without us. Out of sounds, words and other frail and worthless things, we can construct **playthings**—songs and **poems** full of **meaning**, consolation and goodness, more **beautiful** and **enduring** than the grim sport of fortune and **destiny**.

802.

(narrator speaking of Gertrude) She is my friend, and after lonely, **restless** periods, when I emerge from my **silence** with a song or a sonata, it belongs first and foremost to us both.

803.

(narrator speaking) ... in all my **dreams** I hear my **youth** like a wonderful song which now sounds more **harmonious**...

CHAPTER 25
CHRISTMAS HOLIDAY
W. Somerset Maugham

804.

(narrator speaking of Charley) WITH A **JOURNEY** BEFORE HIM...

805.

(narrator speaking of Leslie) ... was inclined to think that it was **art** only that redeemed human existence from meaninglessness...

806.

(Leslie speaking) ... a **feeling** for **art**...

807.

(Charley speaking) There is nothing I want to do in the world more than **paint**.

808.

(narrator speaking about Charley) ... he got into a set interested in the drama and in his first year **wrote** a couple of one-act plays.

809.

(narrator speaking about Charley) He was bent on **adventure**...

810.

(narrator speaking about Charley) ... **wild** and **romantic** experiences in which his **imagination**...

811.

(narrator speaking of Leslie's impressions of Charley) Even Leslie was impressed by the extent of his **reading** and the clearness with which even as a boy he **expressed** himself.

812.

(narrator speaking about Charley) ... he had an **instinctive feeling**...

813.

(narrator speaking about Leslie) Leslie's **ideas** were liberal...

814.

(narrator speaking about Leslie and Venetia) ... to have a real **love** for **beauty**...

815.

(narrator speaking about Charley) ... the **beauty** of a **restless, striving spirit**.

816.

(narrator speaking about Charley) Charley was a good **listener**...

817.

(narrator speaking about Simon) ... Simon poured out his **ideas**...

818.

(Simon speaking to Charley) But it's not only **knowledge** of men and books that I want to acquire… I want to acquire something much harder to come by and more important: an unconquerable **will**.

819.

(Simon speaking to Charley) I think I've always known myself; there's nothing that teaches you what you are like being **alone** in the world…

820.

(Simon speaking to Charley) But my **knowledge** was **instinctive**.

821.

(Simon speaking to Charley) … I shall feel myself as **free** as a bird in the air.

822.

(narrator speaking about Charley) He was an **imaginative youth** and he had **read** many novels.

Creativity Defined

823.

(narrator speaking) … the **silence** had a thrilling quality of awe.

824.

(Lydia speaking to Charley) I don't mind being **alone**, you know. I sometimes come here by myself and sit for hours.

825.

(Lydia speaking to Charley) When I **read** Tolstoi or Dostoievsky…

826.

(Simon speaking to Charley and Lydia) For a while they sat in **silence**.

827.

(Charley speaking to Lydia) You were **feeling** the **music** as **deeply** as I was… I felt that your **emotion** flowed into me and gave mine a richer **intensity**.

828.

(Charley speaking to Lydia) But almost the first thing I liked in you was that you were so **natural**.

829.

(Charley speaking to Lydia) … one **feels** it is a **true expression**… of your **soul**.

830.

(Lydia speaking to Charley) …It's **painted** with pity and **love**.

831.

(Lydia speaking to Charley) … with those simple objects, with his painter's exquisite **sensibility**…

832.

(Lydia speaking to Charley) … he wanted to show you that if you only have enough **love**, if you only have enough sympathy, out of pain and distress and unkindness, out of all the evil of the world, you can create **beauty**.

833.

(Lydia speaking to Charley) She was **silent** and for long stood looking at the little picture.

834.

(Charley speaking to Lydia) But you do seem to **feel** about it very strongly, and I suppose **art** is really a matter of **feeling**.

835.

(Lydia speaking to Charley) … the **spirit** of man and the **beauty** he created.

836.

(narrator speaking of Lydia) … to bring out the **tumult** of its **emotion**…

837.

(Lydia speaking to Charley) No, I shan't be bored. It's not often I have the chance to be **alone**… I can't imagine a greater luxury.

838.

(Simon speaking to Charley) To fulfill myself. To satisfy my creative **instinct**. To exercise the capacities that **nature** has endowed me with.

839.

(narrator speaking of Lydia) … an extreme attention as though she were trying to see into the depths of his **soul**.

840.

(Lydia speaking to Charley) I don't know what I believe, because it's **instinctive**, and how can you describe an **instinct** with words?

CHAPTER 26
THE PICTURE OF DORIAN GRAY
Oscar Wilde

841.

(narrator speaking) The studio was filled with the rich odour of roses...

842.

(narrator speaking) ... whose tremulous branches seemed hardly able to bear the burden of a **beauty** so flame-like as theirs...

843.

(Basil Hallward speaking) It seems to be the one thing that can make modern life **mysterious** or marvelous to us.

844.

(Basil Hallward speaking to Harry) ... every portrait that is painted with **feeling** is a portrait of the **artist**, not of the sitter. The sitter is merely the accident, the occasion. It is not he who is revealed by the

painter; it is rather the painter who, on the coloured canvas, reveals himself… I have shown in it the **secret** of my own **soul**.

845.

(Basil Hallward speaking to Harry) You know we poor **artists** have to show ourselves in society from time to time, just to remind the public that we are not savages.

846.

(Basil Hallward speaking to Harry) … how **independent** I am by nature. I have always been my own master…

847.

(Basil Hallward speaking to Harry) … we were **destined** to know each other.

848.

(Basil Hallward speaking to Harry) The first is the appearance of a **new** medium for **art**, and the second is the appearance of a new personality for art also.

849.

(Basil Hallward speaking to Harry) There is nothing that **Art** cannot **express**, and I know that the **work** I have done...

850.

(Basil Hallward speaking to Harry) ... has suggested to me an entirely **new** manner in **art**, an entirely new mode of style. I see things **differently**, I think of them differently. I can now recreate life in a way that was hidden from me before. A **dream** of form in days of thought...

851.

(Basil Hallward speaking to Harry) a school that is to have in it all the **passion** of the **romantic spirit**... The **harmony** of **soul** and body...

852.

(Basil Hallward speaking to Harry) Some subtle **influence** passed from him to me...

853.

(Basil Hallward speaking to Harry) ... present in my **work**...

854.

(Basil Hallward speaking to Harry) An **artist** should create **beautiful** things… We have lost the abstract sense of beauty.

855

(Basil Hallward speaking to Harry) You can't **feel** what I feel.

856.

(Dorian Gray speaking to Basil Hallward) I want to **learn** them.

857.

(Basil Hallward speaking to Dorian Gray) Because to influence a person is to give him one's own **soul**. He does not think his **natural** thoughts, or burn with his natural **passions**. His virtues are not real to him… He becomes an echo of someone else's **music**, an actor of a part that has not been written for him. The aim of life is **self-development**. To realize one's nature perfectly—that is what each of us is here for. People are afraid of themselves, nowadays. They have forgotten the highest of all duties, the duty that one owes to one's self… But their own souls starve…

858.

(Lord Henry speaking) I believe that if one man were to live out his life fully and completely, were to give form to every **feeling**, **expression** to every thought, reality to every **dream**—I believe that the world would gain such a fresh **impulse** of **joy**... and return to the Hellenic **ideal**...

859.

(Lord Henry speaking) It has been said that the great events of the world take place in the brain.

860.

(narrator speaking of Dorian Gray) ... had touched some **secret** chord that had never been touched before, but that he felt was now vibrating and throbbing to curious pulses.

861.

(narrator speaking of Dorian Gray) **Music** had stirred him like that. Music had **troubled** him many times... It was... another **chaos** that created in us.

862.

(narrator speaking of Basil Hallward) Hallward painted away with that marvelous **bold** touch of his that had the true refinement and perfect delicacy that in **art**, at any rate, comes only from **strength**. He was unconscious of the **silence**.

863.

(Lord Henry speaking to Dorian Gray) Nothing can cure the **soul** but the **senses**, just as nothing can cure the senses but the soul.

864.

(narrator speaking of Dorian Gray) Suddenly there had come some one across his life who seemed to have disclosed to him life's **mystery**.

865.

(Lord Henry speaking to Dorian Gray) And **Beauty** is a form of **Genius**... It is of the great facts of the world, like sunlight, or springtime, or the reflection in dark waters of the silver shell we call the moon... It has its **divine** right of sovereignty.

866.

(Lord Henry speaking to Dorian Gray) To me, **Beauty** is the **wonder** of wonders.

867.

(Lord Henry speaking to Dorian Gray) The true **mystery** of the world is the visible, not the invisible…

868.

(Lord Henry speaking to Dorian Gray) Ah! Realize your **youth** while you have it. Don't squander the gold of your days, listening to the tedious, trying to improve the hopeless failure, or giving away your life to the ignorant, the common, and the vulgar. These are the sickly aims, the false ideas, of our age. Live! Live the wonderful life that is you! Let nothing be lost upon you. Be always **searching** for new **sensations**.

869.

(Lord Henry speaking to Dorian Gray) There is absolutely nothing in the world but **youth**!

870.

(narrator speaking of Dorian Gray) … when we are stirred by some **new emotion**…

871.

(narrator speaking of Dorian Gray) … his **soul** who sought for her there had been wakened that wonderful **vision** to which alone are wonderful things revealed…

872.

(Lord Henry speaking to Lady Agatha, Sir Thomas, and others) One should sympathise with the colour, the **beauty**, the **joy** of life.

873.

(Lord Henry speaking to Lady Agatha, Sir Thomas, and others) … that is one of the great **secrets** of life. Nowadays most people die of a sort of creeping common sense, and **discover** when it is too late that the only things one never regrets are one's mistakes… (narrator speaking about Lord Henry) He **played** with the **idea**, and grew **willful**; tossed it into the air and **transformed** it…

874.

(Lord Henry speaking of Dorian Gray) His nature had **developed** like a flower, had **borne** blossoms of scarlet flame. Out of its **secret** hiding-place had crept his **Soul**, and **Desire** had come to meet it on the way.

875.

(Lord Henry speaking to Dorian Gray) Good **artists** exist simply in what they make…

876.

(narrator speaking) It was true that as one watched life in its curious crucible of **pain** and **pleasure**, one could not wear over one's face a mask of glass, nor keep the sulphurous fumes from **troubling** the brain and making the **imagination** turbid with monstruous fancies and misshapen **dreams**.

877.

(narrator speaking) To note the curious hard logic of **passion**, and the **emotional** coloured life of the **intellect**—to observe where they met, and where they separated, at what point they were in unison, and at what point they were at discord… One could never pay too high a price for any **sensation**.

878.

(narrator speaking of Dorian Gray) ... that it was through certain words of his, **musical** words said with musical utterance, that Dorian Gray's **soul**...

879.

(narrator speaking) Ordinary people waited till life disclosed to them its **secrets**, but to the few, to the elect, the **mysteries** of life were revealed before the veil was drawn away. Sometimes this was the effect of **art,** and chiefly the art of **literature**, which dealt immediately with the **passions** and the **intellect**. But now and then a **complex** personality took the place and assumed the office of art, was indeed, in its way, a real work of art, Life having its elaborate masterpieces, just as **poetry** has, or **sculpture**, or **painting**.

880.

(narrator speaking of Dorian Gray) The pulse and **passion** of **youth** were in him...

881.

(narrator speaking of Dorian Gray) ... his **beautiful soul**...

882.

(narrator speaking of Dorian Gray) … whose **joys** seem to be remote from one, but whose sorrows stir one's **sense** of **beauty**…

883.

(narrator speaking of Dorian Gray) **Soul** and body, body and soul— how **mysterious** they were!

884.

(Sibyl speaking to Jim) To be in **love** is to surpass one's self.

885.

(Harry speaking to Dorian Gray) **Pleasure** is **Nature's** test…

886.

(Harry speaking to Dorian Gray and to Basil Hallward) To be good is to be in **harmony** with one's self… Discord is to be forced to be in harmony with others. One's own life— that is the important thing.

887.

(Lord Henry speaking to Dorian Gray and to Basil Hallward) … I am always ready for a **new emotion.**

888.

(narrator speaking) The **painter** was **silent** and preoccupied.

889.

(Dorian Gray speaking to Sibyl Vane) I loved you because you were marvelous, because you had **genius** and **intellect**, because you realised the **dreams** of great **poets** and gave shape and substance to the shadows of **art.**

890.

(narrator speaking of Dorian Gray) It had taught him to **love** his own **beauty.**

891.

(narrator speaking of Dorian Gray) … his own **infinite curiosity** about life. **Eternal youth, infinite passion, pleasures** subtle and **secret, wild joys…**

892.

(Dorian Gray speaking to Basil Hallward) I have **new passions**, new thoughts, new **ideas**. I am **different**... I am **changed**...

893.

(Basil Hallward speaking to Dorian Gray) ... the visible incarnation of that unseen **ideal** whose memory haunts us **artists** like an exquisite **dream**.

894.

(narrator speaking) Cloudless, and pierced by one **solitary** star, a copper-green sky gleamed through the windows.

895.

(narrator speaking of Dorian Gray) The more he knew, the more he **desired** to know.

896.

(narrator speaking) The worship of the **senses**...

897.

(narrator speaking of Dorian Gray) It was to have its service of the **intellect**, certainly; yet, it was never to accept any theory or system that would involve the sacrifice of any mode of **passionate** experience. Its aim, indeed, was to be experience itself...

898.

(narrator speaking) ... or a **wild longing**, it may be, that our eyelids might open some morning upon a world that had been refashioned **anew** in the darkness for our pleasure, a world in which things would have fresh shapes and colours, and be **changed**...

899.

(narrator speaking of Dorian Gray) ... in his **search** for **sensations** that would be at once **new** and **delightful**, and possess the elements of **strangeness** that is so essential to **romance**, he would often adopt certain modes of thought he knew to be really alien to his nature, abandon himself to their subtle **influences**, and then, having, as it were, caught their colour and satisfied his **intellectual curiosity**, leave them with the curious indifference that is not incompatible with a real **ardour** of temperament...

900.

(narrator speaking of Dorian Gray) He knew that the **senses**, no less than the **soul**, have their spiritual **mysteries** to reveal.

901.

(narrator speaking of Dorian Gray) He saw that there was no mood of mind that had not its counterpart in the **sensuous** life, and set himself to **discover** their true relations...

902.

(narrator speaking of Dorian Gray) At another time he **devoted** himself entirely to **music**...

903.

(narrator speaking) ... Schubert's grace, and Chopin's **beautiful sorrows**, and the mighty **harmonies** of Beethoven...

904.

(narrator speaking of Dorian Gray) ... and he felt a **curious delight** in the thought that **Art**, like **Nature**, has her monsters...

905.

(narrator speaking of Dorian Gray) ... **listening** in **rapt pleasure** to *Tannhäuser*, and seeing in the prelude to that great **work** of **art** a presentation of the tragedy of his own **soul**.

906.

(narrator speaking of Dorian Gray) He **discovered** wonderful stories...

907.

(narrator speaking of Dorian Gray) To him, man was a being with... myriad **sensations**, a **complex** multi-form creature that bore within itself **strange** legacies of thought and **passion**...

908.

(narrator speaking of Dorian Gray) ... his **imagination** had created it for him, as it had been in his brain and **passions**.

909.

(narrator speaking of Dorian Gray) ... they **troubled** his **imagination** in the day.

910.

(narrator speaking of Dorian Gray) … he could realize his conception of the **beautiful**.

911.

(Dorian Gray speaking to Basil Hallward) One day you introduced me to a friend of yours, who explained to me the **wonder** of **youth**, and you finished a portrait of me that revealed to me the wonder of **beauty**.

912.

(narrator speaking of Alan Campbell) …his name appeared once or twice in some of the scientific reviews, in connection with certain **curious experiments**.

913.

(narrator speaking) … the **freedom** of their **will**.

914.

(Lord Henry speaking to Gladys) **Romance** lives by repetition, and repetition converts an appetite into an **art**. Besides, each time that one

loves is the only time one has ever loved. **Difference** of object does not alter singleness of **passion**. It merely intensifies it. We can have in life but one great experience at best, and the **secret** of life is to reproduce that experience as often as possible.

915.

(narrator speaking of Dorian Gray) There was something in the clear, pine-scented air of that winter morning that seemed to bring him back to his **joyousness** and his **ardour** for life.

916.

(Harry speaking to Dorian Gray) But a chance tone of colour in a room or a morning sky, a particular perfume that you had once **loved** and that brings subtle memories with it, a line from a forgotten **poem** that you had come across again, a cadence from a piece of **music** that you had ceased to play—I tell you Dorian, that it is on things like these that our lives depend. Browning writes about that somewhere; but our own **senses** will **imagine** them for us. There are moments when the odour of *lilas blanc* passes suddenly across me, and I have to live the **strangest** month of my life over again.

917.

(Harry speaking to Dorian Gray) Life has been your **art**. You have set yourself to **music**. Your days are your sonnets.

CHAPTER 27
REQUIEM FOR A WOMAN
by Rainer Maria Rilke

918.

For we **transform** these things:

They are not here, but mirrored in to us

From out our being, as we catch sight of them.

919.

That you should loose a piece of your **eternity**

920.

Because you are so certain of yourself

921.

That you walk around, a **child** not yet afraid

922.

Why do you come so **differently**? Why do you **contradict** yourself?

923.

You: who were sweet already in your **senses**.

924.

The many **energies** of your great future

925.

By all the **freedom** that you find in you.

926.

And everywhere we **love,** we have but this:

To let each other go; since holding on

Is easy, and we don't have to learn it first.

927.

And **artists** at their labors sometimes **sense**

That everywhere they **love**, they must **work change**.

928.

Anyone who puts His blood into a lifelong **work** can **find**

BOOKS CITED IN CREATIVITY DEFINED

A Session with Doctor Noir written by Alfred de Vigny (1963) McGill University Press, Montreal

Little Herr Friedemann written by Thomas Mann (1988), *Death in Venice and Other Stories,* Bantam Classic, Bantam Books, New York

The Joker written by Thomas Mann (1988), *Death in Venice and Other Stories,* Bantam Classic, Bantam Books, New York

Tristan written by Thomas Mann (1988), *Death in Venice and Other Stories,* Bantam Classic, Bantam Books, New York

Tonio Kröger written by Thomas Mann (1988), *Death in Venice and Other Stories,* Bantam Classic, Bantam Books, New York

Death in Venice written by Thomas Mann (1988), *Death in Venice and Other Stories,* Bantam Classic, Bantam Books, New York

Eckbert the Fair written by Ludwig Tieck (1998) *Six German Romantic Tales,* Dufour Editions, Chester Springs

The Runemberg written by Ludwig Tieck (1998) *Six German Romantic Tales,* Dufour Editions, Chester Springs

Don Giovanni written by E.T.A. Hoffmann (1998) *Six German Romantic Tales,* Dufour Editions, Chester Springs

The Jesuit Chapel in G. written by E.T.A. Hoffmann (1998) *Six German Romantic Tales,* Dufour Editions, Chester Springs

Women in Love written by D.H. Lawrence (1995) Signet Classic, Penguin Books, New York

For a Night of Love written by Émile Zola (1950) Avon Publishing Company, New York

Hotel du Lac written by Anita Brookner (1984), Vintage Books, Random House, New York

A Closed Eye written by Anita Brookner (1991) Vintage Books, Random House, New York

Doctor Faustus written by Thomas Mann (1997) Vintage Books, Random House, New York

The Flame written by Gabriele D'Annunzio (1991) Quartet Books, New York

Sentimental Education written by Gustave Flaubert (2004) Penguin Classics, Penguin Books, New York

Kallocain written by Karin Boye (1966) The University of Wisconsin Press, Madison

The Virgin and the Gipsy written by D.H. Lawrence (1992) Vintage Books, Random House, New York

The Awakening written by Kate Chopin (1996) Prometheus Books, Amherst

Selected Writings written by Gerard de Nerval (1999) Penguin Classics, Penguin Books, London

Inferno written by August Strindberg (1968) *Inferno, Alone, and Other Writings* Anchor Books, Garden City

Tess of the D'Urbervilles written by Thomas Hardy (2001) Dover Publications, Mineola

Gertrude written by Hermann Hesse (1998) The Noonday Press, New York

Christmas Holiday written by W. Somerset Maugham (2000) Vintage Books, Random House, New York

The Picture of Dorian Gray written by Oscar Wilde (1930) Horace Liveright, New York

Requiem for a Woman written by Rainer Maria Rilke (1981) Threshold Books, Putney

AFTERWORD
WITH MARISOL BLANCO'S POEM "ODYSSEY".

Odyssey

It is there, placidly lying on its bed,
vigorously and frantically pulling you,
calling your name,
with its seductive, mysterious screech,
blue in its existence and promising at least…
You fall for it.

But you look behind
and there you see those, what used to be beautiful eyes.
Now they are just hollow, deeply dead in their glaze,
hopelessly asking you to go and to stay:

Leave and forget me…not.
Please! Go… but do not divide.
Forgive me if I want you to stay,
and forgive me if I want you to leave.

The stillness in you pushes you to choose,
you are in the middle between the ocean and them.
Ahead lies your future, behind lies your past.
What? Go for it! Or become like them.

It is beautiful,
and with its beauty comes its spitefulness…
It is revengeful,
it is omnipotent,
and a back-stabber.

Those eyes, rather,
are honest, pure, and loving.
They are worn and torn from experience,

from what they have seen,
and from their pain,
which you can feel for them.

And still you are,
you cry but your tears are pieces of your heart,
part of you that you leave,
and part of you that you take.
Your life, little by little, melts,
and you try to resist, but you can't.
And at that moment when you decide for one,
the other one cries for you.
It is intense, it is frigid, it is cold-hearted,
that cares nothing about you,
or the souls behind you.

Vividly many memories flood your heart,
you smell them,
you taste them,
you touch them,
you free-fall in them.

But the ocean embellishes you and the eyes…know you can't stay.
Your spirit would disappear in the forgotten essence of the island.
Right now, you cry,
and later on, your eyes would become dry.
Unable to shed a tear,
and hunted by their fears.

The moment comes,
go go quick! Don't look back!
Don't look ahead!
Look back not to forget!
But go, to protect yourself,
and you might be able to return.
Return? You might not see those souls again!
Their time is counted, and their minutes are passing.

*Confused, placid skin
and volcanic heart,
you go into the blue and while closing your eyes,
you search for ways not to regret,
but those eyes, you will never forget.*

-Marisol Blanco

ART BY MARISOL BLANCO

Marisol Blanco, M.S. is a friend and colleague. She has authored poems that affect me deeply.

B.B.
September 2008

CREATIVITY DEFINED INDEX

CREATIVITY KEYWORDS	PASSAGE NUMBERS
absorbed	195, 196, 233, 264, 318, 369, 443, 598
adventures	50, 404, 480, 485, 672, 809
alive/lively	116, 209, 242, 249, 282, 377, 410, 487, 491, 590, 602
almighty	131
alone	12, 65, 86, 98, 221, 229, 348, 365, 390, 449, 455, 582, 735, 819, 824, 837
ardent	1, 182, 202, 654, 727, 782, 784, 899, 915
art/artist	9, 14, 16, 40, 43, 44, 45, 46, 48, 51, 52, 54, 55, 83, 89, 90, 118, 136, 137, 143, 173, 194, 199, 201, 206, 210, 212, 213, 215, 216, 223, 230, 236, 241, 252, 266, 284, 303, 319, 357, 362, 373, 380, 381, 383, 385, 468, 558, 602, 605, 606, 618, 620, 712, 722, 771, 805, 806, 834, 844, 845, 848, 849, 850, 854, 862, 875, 879, 889, 893, 904, 905, 914, 917, 927
artistic thought	139
assert	200, 334
awakened	120, 123, 300, 303, 338, 742
beautiful	1, 10, 16, 50, 52, 53, 55, 57, 63, 85, 115, 116, 138, 152, 174, 177, 200, 207, 212, 217, 218, 225, 235, 235, 241, 242, 252, 267, 277, 292, 298, 299, 321, 360, 379, 386, 441, 480, 486, 519, 572, 586, 602, 604, 612, 620, 656, 674, 688, 739, 757, 758, 766, 772, 801, 814, 815, 832, 835, 842, 854, 865, 866, 872, 881, 882, 890, 903, 910, 911
bold	95, 146, 166, 287, 359, 449, 483, 544, 590, 761, 862
bookish	682

CREATIVITY KEYWORDS	PASSAGE NUMBERS
born/reborn	47, 53, 137, 140, 165, 253, 425, 467, 569, 607, 746, 874
boundless	1, 216, 271, 291, 491
challenges	162
change	218, 355, 595, 622, 674, 892, 898, 927
chaos	25, 438, 578, 861
children/childish	47, 107, 110, 118, 215, 449, 620, 726, 770, 772, 774, 921
complex	175, 879, 907
composer	237, 658
concentration	264, 312, 331, 617, 717
confidence	63, 382, 472, 754
contemplation	432, 438
contradiction	41, 435, 733, 787, 922
controversial	416
courageous	54, 109, 125, 133, 134, 250, 348, 400, 468, 475, 544, 662, 747
creative release	742
creative work	765
Creator	313
curiosity	84, 123, 224, 286, 349, 406, 419, 503, 748, 891, 899
danced	34, 46
daring	50, 114, 133, 340, 395, 450, 468, 481
death	133, 247, 262, 276, 505
deep	47, 51, 61, 66, 71, 203, 224, 297, 349, 370, 394, 528, 566, 626, 791, 827
defiant	54, 166, 423, 468
delight	47, 58, 327, 368, 499, 899, 904
desire	1, 40, 51, 53, 62, 115, 168, 182, 189, 199, 206, 226, 227, 241, 291, 303, 308, 321, 330, 338, 340, 363, 367, 515, 565, 643, 665, 710, 714, 716, 717, 732, 764, 797, 874, 895

CREATIVITY KEYWORDS	PASSAGE NUMBERS
destiny	10, 171, 179, 183, 212, 222, 256, 262, 274, 295, 309, 345, 505, 597, 622, 704, 707, 801, 847
determined	257, 418, 456
development	136, 194, 271, 874
deviated	54
devoted	117, 344, 902
different	63, 158, 302, 321, 401, 519, 639, 753, 850, 892, 914, 922
difficulties	46, 49, 145, 722
disconcerting	50
discover	101, 114, 124, 208, 216, 247, 280, 352, 360, 375, 455, 477, 544, 572, 575, 593, 594, 664, 706, 737, 744, 790, 873, 901, 906
distress	149, 832
divine	1, 131, 220, 235, 259, 277, 284, 317, 523, 529, 549, 616, 770, 865
dreams	68, 100, 115, 118, 167, 177, 188, 200, 207, 210, 211, 212, 253, 286, 293, 303, 350, 354, 356, 360, 381, 436, 455, 482, 484, 498, 503, 510, 518, 520, 527, 530, 542, 543, 544, 546, 551, 569, 609, 645, 648, 709, 718, 761, 770, 772, 773, 781, 803, 850, 858, 876, 889, 893
driven	62, 137
eccentric	135, 475
ecstasy	52, 63, 214, 232, 279, 296, 541, 571, 632, 696, 698
educate	22, 595
effort	49, 137, 172, 199, 219, 234, 242, 252, 312, 331, 340, 546, 568
emancipated	166, 362
emotion	2, 9, 13, 46, 50, 52, 53, 65, 165, 357, 370, 452, 646, 658, 694, 708, 715, 725, 759, 781, 827, 836, 870, 877, 887
enduring/endurance	428, 596, 801

CREATIVITY KEYWORDS	PASSAGE NUMBERS
energy	179, 219, 260, 271, 277, 327, 331, 334, 340, 351, 476, 499, 512, 550, 568, 585, 786, 924
enlightenment	218, 643
escape	51, 91
essence	179, 261, 272, 317, 336, 796
eternity	1, 9, 51, 180, 220, 262, 265, 275, 312, 486, 502, 891, 919
exalt	2, 55, 144, 402, 453, 648, 680, 718, 777, 795
excitement	53, 725
experimenting	334, 573, 634, 912
expression	41, 119, 163, 165, 189, 201, 225, 231, 239, 242, 272, 303, 336, 337, 356, 377, 443, 466, 647, 681, 811, 829, 849, 858
exultation	65, 450
faith	1, 118, 229, 534
fantasy	99, 333, 409, 490, 587, 778
feel	1, 10, 25, 26, 30, 36, 43, 46, 54, 64, 65, 76, 120, 177, 179, 194, 199, 212, 222, 235, 236, 254, 277, 289, 290, 293, 305, 310, 311, 319, 333, 360, 374, 384, 459, 532, 579, 655, 681, 686, 699, 741, 743, 787, 788, 791, 806, 812, 821, 827, 829, 834, 844, 855, 858
fervent	252, 259, 276
focus	334
fortitude	701
free/freedom	12, 29, 78, 83, 87, 92, 101, 115, 128, 129, 130, 141, 147, 165, 190, 208, 224, 235, 240, 254, 337, 341, 342, 346, 351, 353, 391, 396, 434, 459, 545, 550, 574, 580, 635, 637, 667, 706, 721, 733, 735, 740, 775, 791, 821, 913, 925
free-born	425
freethinker	641
fun	613

CREATIVITY KEYWORDS	PASSAGE NUMBERS
genius	12, 26, 42, 137, 144, 181, 223, 229, 267, 336, 357, 381, 486, 563, 599, 722, 865, 889
genuine	444
goals	126, 155, 207, 334, 509, 730, 771
God	4, 9, 52, 373
gods	9, 489, 490, 658, 801
grief	740
harmonious	1, 63, 187, 206, 247, 252, 523, 529, 607, 632, 654, 656, 660, 680, 708, 709, 740, 772, 773, 796, 803, 851, 886, 903
heavenly	9, 152, 510, 707
hero	24, 54, 235, 237, 274, 318, 337, 596
hope	63, 87, 108, 110, 253, 314, 330, 338, 340, 360, 525, 536, 543, 606, 645, 670, 671, 706
idea	10, 120, 159, 194, 201, 207, 225, 235, 269, 271, 315, 317, 358, 389, 428, 503, 506, 527, 540, 578, 620, 629, 639, 732, 813, 817, 873, 892
ideal	27, 174, 179, 199, 206, 209, 228, 231, 234, 252, 255, 274, 278, 313, 327, 331, 340, 344, 386, 486, 492, 519, 614, 644, 649, 723, 858, 893
idle	53, 100, 570
images	25, 50, 177, 190, 195, 199, 202, 207, 209, 210, 215, 221, 231, 243, 290, 292, 303, 306, 317, 321, 335, 340, 511, 521, 527, 531
imagination	9, 13, 15, 54, 111, 131, 150, 170, 185, 187, 207, 218, 272, 277, 297, 316, 332, 379, 384, 444, 446, 476, 479, 499, 539, 781, 798, 810, 822, 876, 908, 909, 916
immortal	178, 252, 271, 314, 324, 340, 366, 529, 534, 554, 697
impatience	224, 282, 339
improve	47, 385, 456
improvise	193, 613, 718

CREATIVITY KEYWORDS	PASSAGE NUMBERS
impulse	137, 222, 238, 309, 435, 638, 691, 694, 698, 699, 858
independence	29, 459, 512, 574, 593, 630, 652, 653, 676, 846
individual/individuality	12, 13, 150, 235, 437, 464, 512, 565, 704, 751
infinite	1, 186, 247, 261, 269, 271, 350, 410, 499, 530, 891
influenced	25, 440, 852, 899
inner breath	372
inner essence	272
inner experiences	24
inner forces	300
inner life	1
inner light	35, 177, 224, 705
inner sight	203
inner struggle	316
inner tumult	196
inner voice	597
innocence	45, 47, 59, 110, 367
insight	1, 6, 34, 202, 733
inspiration	1, 2, 10, 12, 100, 124, 126, 205, 211, 219, 223, 241, 283, 286, 292, 295, 360, 394, 497, 515, 546, 552, 625, 627, 640
instinct	32, 136, 137, 194, 201, 238, 243, 244, 263, 267, 287, 303, 328, 336, 439, 671, 749, 812, 820, 838, 840
intellect	39, 127, 137, 139, 161, 170, 176, 365, 386, 676, 877, 879, 889, 897, 899
intelligence	59, 186, 207, 351, 378, 593
intensity	172, 179, 194, 199, 224, 245, 252, 264, 294, 454, 717, 732, 827
interesting	153, 351, 477
intuition	272, 640

CREATIVITY KEYWORDS	PASSAGE NUMBERS
inventions	162, 186, 267, 500, 588, 618
invincible	671
inward life	439
inward voice	711
irrational	394
journey	118, 485, 655, 672, 804
joy/enjoy	53, 55, 170, 208, 220, 235, 247, 268, 304, 341, 350, 360, 391, 449, 521, 534, 548, 610, 654, 715, 739, 740, 743, 858, 872, 882, 891, 915
knowledge	77, 126, 133, 313, 496, 553, 568, 787, 818, 820
learn	94, 104, 160, 373, 856
liberation	165, 212, 237, 556, 788
liberty	12, 83, 87, 659, 676
listened	35, 264, 310, 313, 458, 599, 816, 905
literature	879
longing	23, 45, 46, 47, 51, 55, 61, 63, 107, 115, 216, 220, 360, 372, 386, 404, 405, 454, 462, 724, 767, 794, 797, 898
love	1, 9, 15, 35, 46, 47, 51, 55, 86, 135, 155, 167, 180, 203, 229, 322, 330, 357, 373, 429, 488, 515, 620, 767, 776, 777, 797, 814, 830, 832, 884, 890, 914, 916, 926, 927
meaning	66, 180, 361, 407, 413, 531, 546, 801
meditation	565, 632, 779, 800
mission	10, 12, 14, 16, 508
muse	10, 213
music	65, 66, 68, 93, 121, 136, 141, 255, 272, 335, 356, 447, 682, 707, 728, 731, 732, 733, 742, 746, 754, 758, 760, 761, 763, 776, 796, 797, 827, 857, 861, 878, 902, 916, 917

CREATIVITY KEYWORDS	PASSAGE NUMBERS
mysterious	1, 39, 64, 66, 71, 135, 174, 179, 194, 201, 202, 220, 235, 247, 265, 269, 272, 284, 288, 292, 299, 300, 312, 317, 322, 424, 428, 499, 504, 507, 514, 528, 529, 538, 577, 594, 709, 843, 864, 867, 879, 883, 900
nature/natural	53, 57, 71, 164, 180, 183, 191, 210, 220, 238, 260, 264, 265, 274, 275, 279, 299, 302, 309, 375, 434, 603, 605, 654, 656, 661, 666, 677, 688, 700, 755, 756, 828, 838, 857, 885, 904
new/renew	60, 64, 75, 78, 104, 122, 141, 151, 154, 156, 159, 162, 172, 174, 195, 205, 212, 258, 266, 267, 279, 292, 311, 319, 336, 412, 456, 467, 490, 491, 525, 545, 583, 586, 598, 605, 606, 671, 673, 679, 684, 689, 728, 743, 775, 792, 848, 850, 870, 887, 892, 898, 899
new-born	467
nourishing	213, 230, 278
novel	146, 685
oblivious	283
obsession	149, 431
obstacles	239, 247, 559
originality	50, 154, 388, 654
overflowing	288
own language	175
own world	707
painful	149, 208, 212, 219, 230, 246, 304, 394, 475, 758, 791, 876
painter/paint	26, 364, 375, 472, 519, 595, 807, 830, 844, 879, 888
paradise	92, 387, 471, 494, 516, 770

CREATIVITY KEYWORDS	PASSAGE NUMBERS
passion	39, 55, 93, 124, 137, 176, 224, 229, 259, 262, 275, 277, 298, 306, 308, 351, 355, 421, 444, 448, 515, 663, 688, 752, 783, 791, 794, 795, 797, 799, 851, 857, 877, 879, 880, 891, 892, 897, 907, 908, 914
path	18, 55, 97, 155, 559, 634, 722, 733, 747, 775, 780
patience	596
peculiar	13, 36, 413, 428
penetrating	50, 196, 202, 247, 371, 378, 453, 514, 528, 529, 581, 654, 728
pensive	60
persist	82, 444, 656
plans	376, 549, 689
playfulness/playthings	73, 118, 801, 873
pleasure	14, 23, 34, 77, 89, 297, 370, 393, 478, 706, 711, 729, 740, 758, 775, 876, 885, 891, 905
poet/poetry	1, 4, 6, 9, 10, 11, 14, 15, 16, 17, 35, 36, 50, 65, 120, 140, 198, 207, 209, 231, 235, 255, 272, 276, 313, 317, 323, 332, 340, 364, 376, 387, 488, 495, 500, 501, 621, 692, 879, 889
power	1, 39, 64, 131, 150, 190, 197, 200, 205, 231, 235, 235, 247, 258, 259, 261, 264, 274, 277, 290, 305, 306, 312, 324, 327, 346, 403, 449, 450, 511, 568, 581, 585, 588, 601, 608, 658, 749, 769, 781
pride	26, 226, 304, 351, 360, 391, 423, 564, 585, 601, 651
privacy	40
produce	10, 16, 48, 49, 53, 83, 131, 137, 140
profound thoughts	654
proud	63, 213, 769
pure	206, 242, 272, 284, 306, 344, 488, 710, 728, 796

CREATIVITY KEYWORDS	PASSAGE NUMBERS
questioning	439
rapture	53
read	25, 58, 120, 135, 315, 351, 352, 360, 456, 473, 628, 629, 677, 678, 811, 822, 825
rebel	5, 147, 198, 246, 281, 683
reflect	36, 38, 60, 109, 526, 532, 639, 669, 681, 687, 729
relentlessly	334, 345, 428
resolute	512, 719
resolve	54, 345, 560, 689, 691, 702
rest	51, 702
restless	316, 781, 802, 815
revelation	68, 571
risks	192
romance	899, 914
romantic	810, 851
sadness	50
sculptor	235, 312, 324, 879
sea/ocean/waves	35, 47, 51, 63, 233, 261, 438, 446, 448, 451, 453
search	61, 186, 241, 292, 385, 453, 469, 485, 527, 561, 702, 750, 868, 899
secret	1, 10, 47, 68, 101, 156, 179, 207, 224, 247, 317, 356, 375, 544, 581, 609, 719, 723, 844, 860, 873, 874, 879, 891, 914
seeks	4, 360, 413
self-confidence	382, 568, 591
self-dedication	372
self-delight	671
self-development	857
self-respect	28

CREATIVITY KEYWORDS	PASSAGE NUMBERS
sensations/senses	23, 112, 129, 247, 297, 303, 317, 322, 328, 365, 413, 444, 462, 544, 578, 585, 622, 626, 629, 654, 663, 673, 690, 710, 716, 739, 863, 868, 877, 882, 896, 899, 900, 907, 916, 923, 927
sensibility	48, 680, 742, 831
sensitivity	175, 176, 217, 310, 422, 752, 793
sensuous	55, 74, 188, 202, 240, 315, 438, 441, 593, 901
silence	40, 50, 60, 96, 196, 221, 234, 235, 248, 252, 262, 272, 296, 301, 306, 315, 320, 324, 338, 344, 346, 367, 392, 557, 584, 640, 679, 687, 802, 823, 826, 833, 862, 888
simplicity	45, 572, 774
sincere	215, 756, 782
singular	224, 717
soaring	1, 550, 654
solitary	53, 188, 214, 565, 659, 894
solitude	12, 14, 50, 56, 58, 60, 107, 114, 164, 270, 344, 363, 438, 446, 451, 488, 513, 523, 532, 557, 584, 642, 734, 736, 764, 789
solutions	162, 717
sorrow	534, 706, 882, 903
soul	1, 33, 34, 55, 59, 63, 64, 88, 163, 167, 179, 195, 206, 212, 213, 235, 246, 252, 261, 265, 279, 288, 295, 303, 311, 318, 320, 326, 329, 346, 364, 366, 370, 371, 391, 438, 448, 450, 468, 501, 529, 534, 550, 557, 578, 603, 623, 625, 626, 645, 665, 693, 699, 731, 740, 791, 829, 839, 844, 851, 857, 863, 871, 874, 878, 881, 883, 900, 905
spirit	12, 53, 55, 64, 67, 68, 69, 166, 174, 198, 216, 252, 271, 276, 277, 298, 337, 338, 344, 453, 462, 563, 607, 632, 656, 671, 696, 815, 835, 851, 900
spontaneous	13, 206, 244, 307, 328, 337, 342

CREATIVITY KEYWORDS	PASSAGE NUMBERS
stimulus	42, 49
strange/stranger	36, 50, 81, 118, 307, 455, 658, 745, 778, 780, 899, 907, 916
strength	71, 169, 183, 207, 226, 235, 241, 246, 259, 279, 283, 285, 298, 302, 308, 347, 391, 420, 464, 499, 505, 706, 708, 742, 744, 782, 791, 862
strive	129, 137, 151, 815
struggle	1, 54, 229, 245, 272, 304, 315, 316, 337, 522, 531, 549, 611, 616, 733
suffering	63, 229, 236, 566, 582, 699, 715, 752, 797
talent	137, 181, 191, 235, 364, 706, 753
tenderness	34, 386, 429
thinking	25, 34, 36, 72, 81, 86, 98, 212, 290, 394, 452, 682, 819, 850
torment	64, 249, 340, 358, 760, 797
transcend	1, 168, 247, 277, 340, 515, 657
transform	64, 174, 177, 179, 203, 219, 220, 261, 264, 524, 873, 918
troubled	249, 316, 356, 861, 876, 909
true expression	829
true self	64
truth	34, 64, 207, 232, 251, 273, 314, 360, 534, 621, 720, 829, 901
tumult	162, 196, 243, 438, 836
uncertainty	589, 712, 780
unconventional	417
unexpected	280, 314, 317, 322, 442, 460, 728
unfamiliar	455, 745
unique	154, 361, 469
unknown	81, 88, 233, 235, 315, 413, 549, 557, 567, 568, 588
unpredictable	491
untraditional	684
urge/urgency	149, 256, 281, 377

CREATIVITY KEYWORDS	PASSAGE NUMBERS
vision	32, 62, 63, 268, 277, 279, 292, 303, 316, 322, 325, 336, 368, 386, 394, 453, 462, 463, 509, 510, 517, 532, 535, 537, 624, 629, 640, 668, 703, 762, 871
visualize	785
voice	10, 70, 235, 238, 284, 317, 438, 597, 599, 679, 711
walk	21, 49, 631
wandered	34, 245, 438, 455, 470, 495, 503, 562
warmth	45, 176
wild	118, 208, 321, 405, 409, 810, 891, 898
will	49, 80, 81, 134, 222, 239, 264, 300, 617, 634, 680, 713, 818, 873, 913
willpower	204, 403, 528, 544
wish	106, 108, 340
wonder	292, 398, 650, 866, 911
work	16, 17, 40, 41, 49, 51, 65, 69, 72, 121, 143, 144, 146, 156, 165, 174, 180, 184, 195, 201, 202, 205, 207, 213, 220, 224, 229, 241, 269, 306, 309, 316, 318, 336, 339, 343, 344, 357, 376, 457, 521, 570, 618, 765, 769, 776, 777, 782, 789, 849, 853, 905, 927, 928
world within	437
writing	30, 34, 36, 49, 53, 120, 140, 188, 309, 339, 343, 355, 389, 394, 397, 472, 508, 584, 587
yearning	157, 349, 372, 430, 784, 797
youthful/young	39, 132, 133, 227, 239, 254, 258, 276, 351, 374, 458, 465, 493, 515, 551, 558, 592, 606, 610, 671, 682, 725, 773, 783, 797, 803, 822, 868, 869, 880, 891, 911

About the Author

Blake Bazel, M.S. Clinical Psychology, is a Creativity researcher. He is the Founder and Executive Editor of *da ek-sistence*, an Existential Psychology and Creativity magazine. Also, his writing has been featured in the Association for Humanistic Psychology's *Perspective* magazine.